We were so inspired reading *Praise Is My Weapon*! Pastor Dan Willis has true revelation of what it means to really praise the Lord. Reading this made us want to praise God. If you want to learn to live a life of praise to get the victory over every area of your life, this is a must-read!

—*Drs. Angelo & Veronica Petrucci*
Three-time Dove Award-winning gospel artists
Founders and pastors, Higher Place Church,
Franklin, Tennessee

From the first time you meet Pastor Dan, you know there's something different about him. He's totally in love with Jesus from the top of his head to the soles of his feet. You can sense that he worships with his whole being—body, soul, and spirit. Pastor Dan has gone through some of life's worst experiences, but he has triumphed in every circumstance through praise. So it is no surprise that he has written a book about the power of praise and worship. As anointed leader, pastor, musician, singer, television host, and author, Dan Willis reveals how we too can defeat the enemy of our souls through the weapon of praise. I am grateful to call him friend, and heartily recommend this unique book!

—*Dr. Garth Coonce*
Founder and president, Total Christian Television Network

DAN **WILLIS**

PRAISE IS MY WEAPON

WHITAKER
HOUSE

Praise Is My Weapon

www.danwillis.org
www.thelighthousechurch.org
Twitter: http://twitter.com/PastorDanWillis
Facebook: http://facebook.com/lhcanations

ISBN: 978-1-62911-339-5
eBook ISBN: 978-1-62911-340-1
Printed in the United States of America
© 2016 by Dan Willis

Whitaker House
1030 Hunt Valley Circle
New Kensington, PA 15068
www.whitakerhouse.com

Library of Congress Cataloging-in-Publication Data

Names: Willis, Dan, author.
Title: Praise is my weapon / by Dan Willis.
Description: New Kensington, PA : Whitaker House, 2016. | Includes
  bibliographical references.
Identifiers: LCCN 2016004205 | ISBN 9781629113395 (trade pbk. : alk. paper)
Subjects: LCSH: Praise of God. | Worship.
Classification: LCC BV10.3 .W555 2016 | DDC 248.3—dc23
LC record available at http://lccn.loc.gov/2016004205

1 2 3 4 5 6 7 8 9 10 11 ⨃ 23 22 21 20 19 18 17 16

DEDICATION

Father God, for giving me a REASON to PRAISE in my struggle.

Linda, for thirty-eight years of walking through dark moments with our hands up, giving God PRAISE. I LOVE you.

Melody, Rachel, Holly, and Chad, my greatest hope in life is that I have taught you that you can PRAISE your way through any storm. I LOVE you.

Mom, thank you for being an inspiration to me, and teaching me how to make it through, by giving HIM ALL of the PRAISE.

Dad, how I PRAISE God for our restoration, I LOVE you.

Renee, thank you for dealing with my madness. I'm sure it has made a PRAISER out of you.

Maddy Banks, your skills in helping this book come together were a true blessing. I PRAISE God for you.

Jonathan, friend and assistant, I PRAISE God for you!

David and the All Nations Choir Bookstore, how I PRAISE God for your spirit of excellence and business management/marketing, all of these 150 years.

Jerome and Juanita, God has given us an amazing ability to frame PRAISE every week together for many years now. I'm so grateful for you.

Sherri, it's an honor to call you daughter.

Skittles (Dan Willis Ministries), folks come and go but you have been steadfast; I am forever grateful.

Pastor Vera Tucker, a PRAISER from way back that every preacher wishes he could preach with.

Pastors Garland and Farida, some of the dearest friends I have, raising up the next generation of PRAISERS.

Lighthouse, thank you my LIGHTHOUSE for never giving up on a man, and staying by my side for thirty-eight years. The joy of my life has been PRAISING God in your four walls.

And to the reader, thank you for taking the time to relive these moments with me. I hope that each journey down this path will help you to gain the PRAISE necessary in overcoming the enemy.

CONTENTS

"He Chose Me"

He chose me; yes, He chose me.
After seeing me at my worst, He came, and He
chose me;
Yes, He chose me; yes, He chose me.
After seeing the worst in me, He found the
best in me.

He made me at my best, and He's seen me at
my worst;
Times He should have walked away, He came
close by my side to stay;
You didn't give up on me but You made me,
Lord, to see;
With love so deep that You should seek to do it
one more time—He chose me.

Now every life must come to the place where
what you've done
Brings bended knee and tears that stream or
cause you to just run;
But His mercy is so free,
Please, don't miss this opportunity, to hear
His words,
"Child, your life I've spared; that you, My
hands can be"

And He loves me.

1

GET TO,
NOT HAVE TO

1

GET TO, NOT HAVE TO

She wore white knee-highs, scuffed-up nursing shoes, white scrubs, and had a wisp of gray hair across her forehead. She shook my hand with such conviction, I wanted to go find the prayer room and get on my face. All she said was, "I really love the Lord," but I felt it to my soul.

Every journey, whether long or short, great or small, must have a starting point. Nothing can be finished that was never started. God's journey of redemption began with one Man, on one cross, for one reason. Romans 5:5–8 says,

> *And hope maketh not ashamed; because the love of God is shed abroad in our hearts by the Holy Ghost which is given unto us. For when we were yet without strength, in due time Christ died for the ungodly. For scarcely for a righteous man will one die: yet peradventure for a good man some would even dare to die. But God commendeth*

his love toward us, in that, while we were yet sinners, Christ died for us.

Do you know why God sent His only begotten Son to us? Why did Christ choose the path of the cross? The answer to these questions is love. Jesus loves us so much more than we can ever comprehend while in this world. So much that He lived a life of pain, rejection, and suffering; so much that He lived a life without sin because He knew that, one day, He would have to willingly offer Himself up as a living sacrifice for all mankind, and in so doing, free even those who hate Him from an eternity of suffering. Who does that? What kind of person willingly dies so that his enemy might be saved? A Savior who loves unconditionally—that's Jesus.

> It was Jesus who took the first step in pursuing a relationship with us, and now He wants us to follow up with Him and make it a two-way relationship.

Wow, this Jesus sounds great! How can you get to known Him? Where do you start? We all start by asking Him for forgiveness and inviting Him into our hearts. The Bible tells us that we love Him because He first loved us. (See 1 John 4:19.) It was Jesus who took the first step in pursuing a relationship with us, and now He wants us to follow up with Him and make it a two-way relationship. You might have already made that step, and now you're asking, "How do I know if I love Him?" Jesus tells us in John 14:15, *"If ye love me, keep my commandments."* It's that simple! You will know you love Him when you keep His commandments! Now that we know the requirements, and who we are, perhaps some of you are wondering if there is anybody who just loves Jesus.

Crazy Love

In my thirty-five years of pastoring, I've been in quite a few of what I call "beat-you-up" churches, the kind where you go in expecting a refreshing encounter with God but come out feeling more defeated than when you entered. I'm sure that everyone has encountered one of these churches at some point in his life. One time, when I went into a church to hear a word, the next thing I knew, the pastor was having everyone look at each other, screaming, "Repent, or you'll go to hell!" Honest to goodness, that actually happened to me!

See, beloved, you can use fear only to scare the hellfire out of someone for so long. At the end of the day, only one thing will ever keep a person going with Christ, and that's love. In a marriage, a man can scare or threaten his wife into staying with him for only so long. One day, he will awake from sleep feeling a little less of a man because she has removed his manhood, as we have seen in the news a few times.

Everybody wants to be loved with a special and unique love. Wouldn't you be crazy to *not* want to be loved this way? Love does have its perks, and, of course, there are many physical aspects of love. In fact, it's said that "events occurring in the brain when we are in love have similarities to mental illness."[1] Love causes flushed cheeks, a racing heart, clammy hands, loss of appetite, and a need for less sleep.[2] See? You *aren't* crazy! That's just love, and isn't it a wonderful thing? Now that you know the effects of love, I want to ask again, is there anybody who just loves Jesus?

"Do You Love Me?"

In John 21 there is a short conversation between Peter and Jesus. Jesus asks Peter a question. He didn't ask him about his works, his thoughts, or his sins. Instead, He asks him the same question three times: *"Lovest thou me?"* (John 21:15–17). The question wasn't profound or mind-boggling. Jesus was simply asking Peter about the nature of his love. The most important thing to Jesus was whether or not He was being loved back.

We are shown here that the very foundation of Christianity and the church is based on love. The church has so many agendas and assignments—issues of labor, racism, tradition, and so forth—and all the while, the number one question Jesus asks is, "Do you love Me?" There are so many folks out there who try to defend Jesus—they blog about Him and fight for Him—but He is a conqueror who needs no defense. He could have called down ten thousand angels to His rescue. (See Matthew 26:53.) He is Truth, and the Truth needs no defense. He doesn't want someone to defend Him; He wants someone to love Him. He wants us to focus on the very thing that brought Him to us and us to Him—love.

---

1. "The Science of Love," *BBC Science: Human Body & Mind*, http://www.bbc.co.uk/science/hottopics/love/.
2. Ibid.

The church has so many agendas and assignments—issues of labor, racism, tradition, and so forth—and all the while, the number one question Jesus asks is, "Do you love Me?"

What does it mean to just love Jesus? It means taking a "want to" approach and not a "have to" approach. Do you feel like you *have* to go church, *have* to praise Him, *have* to worship Him, and *have* to present your body as a sacrifice? (See Romans 12:1.) If you feel that way about praising and worshipping Him, then you shouldn't do it. Don't you know that God loves a cheerful giver? (See 2 Corinthians 9:7.) Not a resentful giver, a grudging giver, or a suspicious giver. You can be moved to give if it's not for love, but any other motivation that love will be only temporary. Occasionally, one of our four kids used to ask, "Dad, do I have to go to church tonight?" I would enthusiastically reply, "No, you *get* to go!" I wanted them to know that a relationship with God is not "have to"; it's "get to"!

What does it mean to love Jesus? It means you want to make Him happy, not because of what He can do for you, but because of who He is. If He never does anything aside from saving you, He is still worthy of your praise. It's not about what He can do for us, but who He is as our Savior. Just as you want to be loved, Jesus still asks us today, *"Lovest thou me?"* Remember, we don't have to give tithes, offerings, time, or resources; we *get* to, just because we really love the Lord!

2

SO MANY
QUESTIONS
BUT NOT MANY
ANSWERS

2

SO MANY QUESTIONS BUT NOT MANY ANSWERS

At 3 AM Monday morning, my wife awakened me from a deep sleep. "Honey, your phone is ringing. Answer your phone."

Who could be calling at this hour? What would he or she have to say? No call at this time of day could bring good news. Hesitating, I slowly reached over and picked up the phone. "Hello?"

It was my close friend of twenty-five years. "Dan, are you sitting down? I hope you're sitting down. I have some terrible news." My heart began to beat faster. "Dan, Mark was killed last night after he got home from church. He was murdered."

Mark was also a close friend of ours for the past twenty-five years. He was a man with whom we had worked, ministered, traveled the world, and become close friends. I began weeping intensely. Shocked, stunned, and horrified, I sat wrapped in a blanket in a cold sweat. Questions began racing through my mind. I tried to form sentences, but my mind wasn't processing quickly enough to articulate my thoughts. Finally, the most logical sentence came through "Are you sure it was him?" Then the next thought, *Who did it?*

A mind filled with unanswered questions is a heavy thing to bear. I cried; I questioned, over and over. Five hours later, I would receive the answers to my questions. I learned that Mark had been stabbed to death by one of his very own family members. It was the most horrifying murder I have ever heard of! My answer had come, but when it had, I was still empty and devastated. It wasn't enough.

Questioning God

One of the greatest men in the Bible was familiar with questions. David had asked over two hundred questions in his lifetime, and they weren't just to anybody and everybody. We find that the majority of documented questions he had asked were directed to God. Who ever said that we couldn't question the Lord? One of David's greatest times of questioning God is found in Psalm 13. He said,

> *How long wilt thou forget me, O Lord? For ever? How long wilt thou hide thy face from me? How long shall I take counsel in my soul, having sorrow in my heart daily? How long shall mine enemy be exalted over me? Consider*

and hear me, O LORD my God: lighten mine eyes, lest I sleep the sleep of death; lest mine enemy say, I have prevailed against him; and those that trouble me rejoice when I am moved. But I have trusted in thy mercy; my heart shall rejoice in thy salvation. I will sing unto the LORD, because he hath dealt bountifully with me.

In this short psalm, David questioned God four times. What was David hoping to gain by asking so many questions? Typically, questions are indicative of a desire to know something or someone, and the normal response is an answer. Getting answers to our questions, though, is all about our approach.

Our approach to God should always be one of thanksgiving. Without that, we inhibit ourselves from any progress, and certainly any answers.

We can't come before God asking in the flesh and expect a spiritual revelation. Imagine this: A man is eating dinner, when two hungry men approach him. The first person comes to him and kindly says, "Sir, I haven't eaten in two days. May I please share that with you?" The second person approaches him and says, "Hey, let me have some of that. I'm hungry!" To whom is he most likely to offer his food? The first man!

This is how we should approach God when we ask

Him a question. Furthermore, the Bible tells us, *"Enter into his gates with thanksgiving, and into his courts with praise: be thankful unto him, and bless his name"* (Psalm 100:4). At the end of Psalm 13, David does exactly that: *"I will sing unto the Lord, because he hath dealt bountifully with me"* (Psalm 13:6). He knew that you don't come into someone's presence or territory demanding answers. Instead, the key is to come in with a thankful heart. Our approach to God should always be one of thanksgiving. Without that, we inhibit ourselves from any progress, and certainly any answers.

The morning after receiving the terrible news about my dear friend, I went straight to my piano. I was hurting to the very core of my soul. I knew of nothing else to do. In my pain, I began to sing and worship. I started praising and trusting Him, and it started with giving thanks. Once I started thanking the Lord, then I could enter into praise and worship, which walked me through my answered and unanswered questions. Sometimes, the answers come, but they bring no relief. However, Christ, who has risen from the dead, is there to walk with you through the valley of the shadow of death. (See Psalm 23:4.) When answers aren't enough, there's Jesus. Call on His name!

"Willing"

If His Word will be sung,
We must do the singing;
If His prayer will be prayed,
We must do the praying;
And if His voice will be heard;
We must do the speaking.

It's not what we say but what we are
That the world sees of Him;
We must be real.

If His love will be shown,
We must do the loving;
If His life be displayed,
We must do the living;
And if His hands must touch man,
We must do the reaching.

Here I am, send me;
I will go.

Willing to go, in spite of what I know;
Willing to do, because I love You;
Willing to teach, so all can be reached;
Not my will, but Your will be done.
From my lips, let praises be sung
You died on the cross,.
For me you gave Your life;
The least I can do for You is sacrifice.

So today, it must be preached.
And Lord, I will do the preaching;
And Lord, Your strength, somebody needs;
Please help me reach them.

Lord, Your work must be done,
So Lord, until You come
Here am I, I'm willing;
Here am I, I'm able;
Here am I, send me, I will go.
I will go.

3

UNSHAKEABLE
CONQUERORS

3

UNSHAKEABLE CONQUERORS

Everyone will be shaken in his or her lifetime. Whether it be in health, finances, love, children, or faith, it doesn't matter. If the devil knows he can get you to question, then be prepared to be shaken. The book of Hebrews tells us that in the last days, everything that can be shaken will be shaken. (See Hebrews 12:26–27.) This is because the devil knows that he is running short on time. He has become so desperate that he will do anything to wear people out and to keep them from the kingdom of heaven.

We Are Unshakeable

The only way to make it through times like these is to make up your mind that you are going to be unshakeable!

How do we become unshakeable? We become unshakeable by first learning to be still. Being still does not mean doing nothing. It means doing something but keeping your mouth shut. Psalm 27:14 says, *"Wait on the LORD: be of good courage, and he shall strengthen thine heart: wait, I say, on the LORD."* I've seen too many folks do nothing in their walks with God and say that they are "being still." Other folks know how to be still but give everybody a piece of their mind. You can only give away so much of your mind before you completely lose it! When we learn to be still, then certain things start happening. First, the details begin to fade away. That man with the purple shirt and black pants who left you starts to become the man who was poorly dressed and then a man you don't even remember. Your need for vengeance is lost.

David was a popular man, while Saul was hated. Saul eventually developed jealousy and wanted David dead; in fact, he attempted to kill David on several occasions. But David refused to retaliate. And the Lord made David the musical comforter to his enemy. David had a "put up and shut up" mentality. His response to Saul's threats was, "I trust God; therefore, I will protect God's anointed one." During all his wounds and pain, he never disengaged from his duties. While wounded, David still won battles.

I remember receiving a terrifying call about my son one spring afternoon. He was in the military and on active duty in Afghanistan. The phone rang, and the person on the other end said, "Sir, your son has been injured. Please stand by for twenty-four hours until we can fill you in on the details."

I panicked inside! How was I supposed to wait for answers concerning my boy? Forty-eight grueling hours later, my son was finally allowed to contact me. The answers had come: he had suffered a broken leg while out in the field. With huge relief, I asked him, "When will you be coming home? What day and what time does your plane arrive?" Surely they would be letting him come back, since he was incapable of fighting.

"Dad," my son said, "I'm not on vacation; I am in a war. They've just reassigned me to light duty until I am healed. They said, 'Keep moving,' because inactivity creates a closed wound, which could lead to a blood clot and death."

You see, so many Christians just become inactive when they are wounded. "I'll get back to church when I get this figured out." Silly rabbit, tricks are for kids! You aren't coming back. Why would you leave what you need the most when you are wounded? This mind-set kills off so many Christians in their walk with God. We need to continue on, press on, and move, lest we die!

No one said it better than Job: "*Though he slay me, **yet will I trust in him: but I will maintain mine own ways before him***" (Job 13:15). Anyone familiar with English grammar is aware that the word "*yet*" is a coordinating conjunction that joins two or more items of equal syntactic value. Now, "*maintain*" means that we are to continue on, or as I say it, "Keep on keepin' on," or as an old friend of mine use to say, "Stay with it!" So, what we get is what we maintain! What Job was really saying to God was not, "Lord, if Your decision is to take my life, I will trust You." Instead he was saying, "Lord, You are doing something greater than just taking my life, You are going beyond slaying me, and the challenge is whether or not I continue to walk with You."

> I am not moved by what I think; I stand on what I know. I am not moved by what I feel; I stand on what I know. I am not moved by what I hear; I stand on what I know.

This is the attitude we should have when we come into His presence. How many times do people get distracted or removed from the Spirit because they allow themselves to be shaken by the question, "Is this from God?" Don't be shaken by what's going on around you.

I met a man who told me this funny but true story about what happened shortly after he was converted and received the Holy Spirit. He was approached by a man who told him that speaking in tongues was of the devil.

Dumbfounded, I looked at him and said, "I used to be the worst sinner; I wanted to try everything. If you're telling me that tongues is of the devil, then I'm upset because I didn't get that gift when I was trying to be the worst devil there was."

These are just simple tactics of the enemy to move us. He knows that when one is moved, then instability can arise. It's as simple as this: if something is good, then it is of God; if it's bad, then it is of the devil. It's that simple!

I have had to learn to be unshakeable, and here is the key: I am not moved by what I think; I stand on what I know. I am not moved by what I feel; I stand on what I know. I am not moved by what I hear; I stand on what I know. "On Christ the solid Rock I stand"![3]

We Are "More Than" Conquerors

One day while reading the Bible, I was led to a few particular verses in Romans:

> *Who shall separate us from the love of Christ? shall tribulation, or distress, or persecution, or famine, or nakedness, or peril, or sword?…Nay, in all these things we are more than conquerors through him that loved us. For I am persuaded, that neither death, nor life, nor angels, nor principalities, nor powers, nor things present, nor things to come, nor height, nor depth, nor any other creature, shall be able to separate us from the love of God, which is in Christ Jesus our Lord.* (Romans 8:35, 37–39)

Instantly, I had a revelation that we are not merely conquerors but more than conquerors. Following this, I decided to research the word conqueror and found that this is the only time it is used in the Bible. Further study revealed what exactly a conqueror is—one who takes by force and subdues an enemy; overcoming by confrontation, force, elimination, killing, and fear.

What exactly are we conquerors of? A key phrase in the Scripture passage is *"in all these things."* Not "after all of these things" or "in some of these things" but *"in all these things."* What are these things that we conquer? Tribulation, distress, persecution, famine, nakedness, peril, and sword. Even while

3. Edward Mote, "My Hope Is Built on Nothing Less," 1836.

Tribulation, distress, persecution, famine, nakedness, peril, and sword. Even while you are experiencing these things, you are more than a conqueror.

you are experiencing these things, you are more than a conqueror.

There is a difference between a conqueror and a "more than" conqueror. A conqueror is constantly fighting. He attains victory, but it lasts only as long as his strength and power hold out. Even a shark battling a fisherman will eventually give out. The enemy knows it's more than a physical battle; it's also mental. Have you ever had trouble with your finances, and then your health, your children, and so on? Perhaps it seemed like the enemy just wouldn't leave you alone, and everything that could go wrong did go wrong.

In these instances, a "more than" conqueror knows that the weapons of his warfare are not carnal. Don't just conquer your finances, health, and so forth, because they will come back. To be a "more than" conqueror, you need to face the spirits controlling your finances, health, marriage, and so forth. But fighting these spirits alone will only cause failure. We need the Holy Spirit!

Everything has a purpose, so what exactly is the purpose of conquering? Simply put, conquering increases our territory. In 1 Chronicles, Jabez said, *"Oh that thou wouldest bless me indeed, and enlarge my coast…and that thou wouldest keep me from evil, that it may not grieve me!"* (1 Chronicles 4:10). Jabez knew something very critical about increasing territory—mainly, that it allows for an increased harvest. You see, a vineyard can't be planted in a pot; but when we acquire a field, then we are ready to start planting our vineyard. We must remember, though, that the larger our territory, the larger the area for the enemy to attack, because every inch of kingdom soil is contested. *"The kingdom of heaven suffereth violence, and the violent take it by force"* (Matthew 11:12). So don't ask for more if you can't learn to be a "more than" conqueror, because your strength will fail. Scripture says, *"Not by might, nor by power, but by my spirit, saith the Lord of hosts"* (Zechariah 4:6).

Notice that I left out verse 36 in the Scripture passage at the beginning of the chapter, because it seemed to flow more naturally without it. But now let's take a look at it now:

> For thy sake we are killed all the day long; we are accounted as sheep for the slaughter.

This verse seems so out of place, but a close examination reveals that this is what "more than" conquering is all about. Jesus came and died all because of love. Remember, He could have called down ten thousand angels and slaughtered the men who brought Him to the cross. (See Matthew 26:53.) What would this have accomplished though? Praise God He didn't! A "more than" conqueror doesn't engage the enemy; instead, he takes control and engages the spirit behind the enemy.

A "more than" conqueror doesn't engage the enemy; instead, he takes control and engages the spirit behind the enemy.

Had Jesus summoned the angels, He would have only defeated the enemy. Because He didn't, He conquered the enemy and provided propitiation for our sins. As a result, we are now able to live under grace and be joint-heirs with Christ. Take control! We have authority in Him.

In taking control it is necessary to take up the whole armor of God—not some of it, but all of it.

Wherefore take unto you the whole armour of God, that ye may be able to withstand in the evil day, and having done all, to stand. Stand therefore, having your loins girt about with truth, and having on the breastplate of righteousness; and your feet shod with the preparation of the gospel of peace; above all, taking the shield of faith, wherewith ye shall be able to quench all the fiery darts of the wicked. And take the helmet of salvation, and the sword of the Spirit, which is the word of God.

(Ephesians 6:13–17)

The whole armor is needed not so much for open hand fighting but for protection even when we can't see what's coming. It's more for defense than offense. Don't put on the whole armor just so you can subdue, but so you can stand. We wrestle not against flesh and blood (see Ephesians 6:12), but flesh and blood wrestle against us.

4

DECLARE AND
DECREE

4

DECLARE AND DECREE

A decree is a rule of law issued by the head of state. Let's say France and England are warring over a remote territory. Now, if England wins the war, it gains that territory, which then is officially under British law. Think of the spiritual world and God's kingdom this way. They are constantly at war. When we as children of God take control and enlarge our territory, we as legal authorities in the kingdom of heaven have every right to decree God's Word over that area. And God's Word will not return to Him void. (See Isaiah 55:11.) *"God is not a man, that he should lie"* (Numbers 23:19).

Who is God? Quite a broad and impossible question to answer, right? Especially given the fact that we are tackling an infinite subject matter by finite means. Fortunately, the Bible gives us clues to help us assimilate an answer, such as the many names for God. There are well over one hundred names for

God mentioned in the Bible, and each name gives us a facet of who He is. Whatever God has been or will be for you is just a minute piece of the puzzle of who He is. If we compiled who God has been for every individual who ever existed into one whole, we still wouldn't be able to scratch the surface of who He is or comprehend Him.

> We have to know who He is so we know what He can do. Our knowledge of this scares the devil. When you know who God is, then you can begin to declare and decree who He is in your life.

Why do we have to know who God is? We have to know who He is so we know what He can do. Our knowledge of this scares the devil. When you know who God is, then you can begin to declare and decree who He is in your life. After all, isn't that one of the main reasons we praise and worship God? It's to honor Him. Lord, You are Jehovah-Jireh, Jehovah-Tsidkenu, Alpha and Omega, King of Kings, and Lord of Lords. Luke 1:37 tells us, *"For with God nothing shall be impossible."* He is a God of the impossible. All things, not some things, *all things* are possible through Him and with Him. Start declaring and decreeing who He is in your life, then watch as doors open, situations shift, and miracles manifest.

You Can't Out Give God

I remember one weekend when the Holy Spirit told me to take a love offering for one of our dear members whose family was going through some struggles at the time. Being obedient, I did as He had told me to do. Following church services that weekend, I was immediately attacked by the enemy, who taunted, "What now, pastor? You're in the middle of a building project, and you're having the church give away the funds that you need?"

Immediately, the Lord told me to start declaring and decreeing that the five thousand dollars we had just raised for the family would be given back to us in more donations. So I began to do that; I spoke it every single day and began expecting to hear from our accounting department. One day, two days, three days, and then four days passed by. I continued to praise and worship God, thanking Him and decreeing that the money would come. Five days later, my assistant came to me and said, "Dan, your next guest is here. They are urgently asking to speak with you. They have something important for you."

Now, you have to understand that typically, guests wait in a green room before meeting with me, and any communication before the Sunday service is usually limited due to time. However, I felt in my spirit that I was supposed to meet with this person. So I went to the green room and encountered a very excited person anxiously jumping up and down. "Pastor Dan! I couldn't wait to get here! I have something for you. I was going to wait and give this to you next month, but the Holy Spirit said I was to bring it to you today."

Every time you confess failure and weakness, you unknowingly magnify (praise) Satan above God. Scripture says that we are to *"hold fast our profession"* (Hebrews 4:14). Stand by your declaration of faith through thick and thin, through sunny days and the storms of life.

Then I was handed a cashier's check. I opened it and, to my shock, read $30,000! In five days, the Lord had turned a $5,000-seed our congregation had sowed to a needy family into $30,000! What I learned was this: You can't out give God!

I had taken control of the situation; therefore, I could boldly come before God declaring and decreeing in Jesus' name. I knew that my petition would be heard. I was simply following the principle outlined at the beginning of this chapter. Because God's law was dominating, it had to come to pass. Remember, we must declare it every day. If it still doesn't happen, declare it again!

What is your declaration of faith? Too often we declare our faith and then ruin it by confessing an "opt out" clause. When the sky is blue and the sun is shining, our declarations of faith are strong and vigorous. But when the storms come, we allow doubt to creep in. You may experience pain and confess, "By His stripes I am healed!" (See Isaiah 53:4–5.) Then in your next breath you mutter, "Maybe God wants me to suffer through this pain." In reality, you made two declarations there. In the first, you made a profession of divine healing and redemption in Christ, but in the second, you admitted that redemption and healing were not a fact. You see, you cannot one minute declare, "My God shall supply my every need" (see Philippians 4:19) and then follow it up with, "Yeah, He supplies my needs but I still can't pay the phone bill and the cable got cut off."

Every time you confess failure and weakness, you unknowingly magnify (praise) Satan above God. Scripture says that we are to *hold fast our profession* (Hebrews 4:14). Stand by your declaration of faith through thick and thin, through sunny days and the storms of life. When you talk only about your trials and difficulties, your spirit life shrinks. Instead, when you speak of almighty God and what He can do, fill your lips with praise for answers to prayers that you have made to Him. Your faith will grow by leaps and bounds. What declaration of faith are you holding fast?

"You Always Come Through for Me"

You always come through for me,
Whenever I am in need;
I've never spent one night alone,
Since You came to me.

I traveled so long, so far from Your arms;
I didn't think anything mattered
Since heartache and pain always whistled
my name;
My worth was totally shattered;

But one night, You came, calling me out
by name;
The only thing that suddenly mattered
was to hear those words
"You are free at last; your past life has all
been forgotten."

You always come through for me,
Whenever I am in need;
I've never spent one night alone,
Since You came to me.

5

WHAT IS
PRAISE?

5

WHAT IS PRAISE?

The word *praise* is used two hundred forty-eight times in the Bible. Praise means to magnify, glorify, and exalt the Lord for what He has done. Worship, on the other hand, is more about giving to God for who He is.

In the Old Testament, the word *praise* was strictly used in reference to offerings—sacrifices of turtledoves, bullocks, and goats. The definition of praise would grow with each generation, until we see David say, *"Enter into his gates with thanksgiving, and into his courts with praise: be thankful unto him, and bless his name"* (Psalm 100:4). David knew that praise had to come first; praise gets us into God's courts.

Praise Is Our Weapon

Why exactly do we praise the Lord? Well, first, praise is our weapon, and it comes in many forms, including but not limited to making music, singing, dancing, writing poetry, giving offerings, and speaking the Word. Jesus quoted the Word as a praise weapon. One of the best examples of this is found in Revelation 19:15:

> *And out of his mouth goeth a sharp sword, that with it he should smite the nations: and he shall rule them with a rod of iron: and he treadeth the winepress of the fierceness and wrath of Almighty God.*

Remember, we learned that a "more than" conqueror is one who engages the spirit of the battle, and that the whole armor is not solely for offense but for defense, for protection.

> Clapping our hands in praise to Him is spiritual warfare! We must get rid of all ambiguity because this is not a carnal fight; it's a spiritual battle.

So while you're standing ground, engage the spirit. After all, this is a fight. In fact, 2 Timothy 4:7 says that it is *"a good fight,"* but only if you win. So how exactly do you fight a *"good fight"*?

First, you have to understand that a *"good fight"* doesn't mean an ugly fight; that would lead only to a more militant religion, and there are already plenty of those. The danger is that many people misinterpret verses like Matthew 11:12, which says, *"The kingdom of heaven suffereth violence, and the violent take it by force.*" We need to look at verses like Psalm 144:1, which reads, "*Blessed be the* LORD *my strength which teacheth my hands to war, and my fingers to fight.*" Our hands are instruments and weapons. Have you ever seen a drummer war with his hands or a pianist fight with his fingers? This is what the Bible means by warring with hands and fighting with fingers. Clapping our hands in praise to Him is spiritual warfare! We must get rid of all ambiguity because this is not a carnal fight; it's a spiritual battle. You need to know how to engage in holy fighting, which brings peace and victory, rather than ugly fighting, which leads to confusion and loss.

> *Who shall go up for us against the Canaanites first, to fight against them? And the* LORD *said, Judah shall go up.*   (Judges 1:1–2)

> *And the children of Israel arose, and went up to the house of God, and asked counsel of God, and said, Which of us shall go up first to the battle against the children of Benjamin? And the* LORD *said, Judah shall go up first.*
>   (Judges 20:18)

It appears that whenever the children of Israel would go into battle, God would have the tribe of Judah go in first. Why was this? Well, *Judah* means "praise," so what the Lord shows us is that praise should go first into any battle. This is one reason most churches start their services with praise, because it causes the enemy to flee! If you are new to a Spirit-filled church, maybe you don't understand why the pastor doesn't just come in and start teaching; it's because the Bible says that when you're going into battle, Judah should go first. *Praise should go first.*

> The devil does not know how to react when you come to church even when everything feels like it's coming down on you, or coming against you, and yet you put your purse down, take your coat off, raise your hands to God, and praise Him.

At our church, we start every single service with the music, with praise. We start with praise, clapping our hands, lifting our hands, singing to the Lord, and playing the instruments. Why does praise need to go first? Because it confuses, or confounds, the enemy. The devil does not know how to react when you come to church even when everything feels like it's coming down on you, or coming against you, and yet you put your purse down, take your coat off, raise your hands to God, and praise Him. The devil starts calling a meeting with other hosts of hell, saying, "How come she's praising God? Everything we did to her, she ought not to be praising God like that."

Now, what about the people who get to church late? Sometimes, people will say to me, "I was late to church, but I got there in time to hear the Word." I understand what they are saying, but I am going to say it like it is: this is flattery. I'm grateful that these people are getting the Word, but if they were late, they missed the choir, they missed the praise. They say that they got what they needed, but did they give to God what He needed? Don't just say that you got your Word and that's all you need. God's been waiting for you to enter into His gates with praise.

When you were in your mother's womb, God said, "I had thoughts of peace and not evil toward you." (See Jeremiah 29:11.) God has plans for your life. He said that there would be miracles, signs, and wonders in the last days, and I am here today to tell you that your miracles have already been spoken by God! Perhaps they haven't yet manifested because you haven't yet learned how to praise God.

Nothing tells the story of the weapon of praise like the story in 2 Chronicles 20, in which Judah faced a large army and was quite overwhelmed:

> *O our God, wilt thou not judge them? for we have no might against this great company that cometh against us; neither know we what to do: but our eyes are upon thee.*
> (2 Chronicles 20:12)

Judah brought 1,160,000 soldiers to war. I did a little research, and discovered that this would be like the entire South Side of Chicago as an army. That's a lot of people— grandmas, grandpas, moms, dads, kids—all of them. But then, historians say, as big as the army Jehoshaphat was, the enemy was even bigger, and may have been as big as the populations of California, New Mexico, and Nevada combined. So many in number that when they came out, there was no way that Judah's 1,160,000 could even go against them. They were no match for the enemy. This is why it was all fun and games until the enemy started coming off the boats, and then they said, "God, we don't know what to do, but our eyes are upon you." (See verse 12.)

Now, historians also say that Judah had about four thousand musicians and singers; one hundred twenty cymbals and trumpets; and hundreds of dancers, and they all were to go in before the army. No wonder the leaders consulted with the people first, because if this didn't go right, the singers would go to heaven first! Let's look at more of the passage:

> *Then upon Jahaziel the son of Zechariah, the son of Benaiah, the son of Jeiel, the son of Mattaniah, a Levite of the sons of Asaph, came the Spirit of the LORD in the midst of the congregation; and he said, Hearken ye, all Judah, and ye inhabitants of Jerusalem, and thou king Jehoshaphat, thus saith the LORD unto you, Be not afraid nor dismayed by reason of this great multitude; for the battle is not yours, but God's. To morrow go ye down against them: behold, they come up by the cliff of Ziz; and ye shall find them at the end of the brook, before the wilderness of Jeruel. Ye shall not need to fight in this battle: set yourselves, stand ye still, and see the salvation of the LORD with you, O Judah and Jerusalem: fear not, nor be dismayed; to morrow go out against them: for the LORD will be with you. And Jehoshaphat bowed his head with his face to the ground: and all Judah and the inhabitants of Jerusalem fell before the LORD, worshipping the LORD. And the Levites, of the children of the Kohathites, and of the children of the Korhites, stood up to praise the LORD God of Israel with a loud voice on high. And they rose early in the morning, and went forth into the wilderness*

of Tekoa: and as they went forth, Jehoshaphat stood and said, Hear me, O Judah, and ye inhabitants of Jerusalem; Believe in the LORD your God, so shall ye be established; believe his prophets, so shall ye prosper. And when he had consulted with the people, he appointed singers unto the LORD, and that should praise the beauty of holiness, as they went out before the army, and to say, Praise the LORD; for his mercy endureth for ever. And when they began to sing and to praise, the LORD set ambushments against the children of Ammon, Moab, and mount Seir, which were come against Judah; and they were smitten.

(2 Chronicles 20:14–22)

Praise is what
manifests
the promises
of God! The
victory is in
the Word of
God!

Judah brought an army, so it was quite obvious they expected a battle. However, they also brought singers, so it was quite obvious they expected a supernatural victory! The victory was promised in Jahaziel's prophetic word but manifested during the praise of the singers! Praise is what manifests the promises of God! The victory is in the Word of God!

The children of Israel knew that the battle was too great. What could they do? They were defenseless and had no options. Not only was that the case for the children of Israel, but it also holds true for us today. How many of you know that, no matter what, God is always an option?

Look at the three things that happened in Psalm 9:1–3:

I will praise thee, O LORD, with my whole heart; I will shew forth all thy marvellous works. I will be glad and rejoice in thee: I will sing praise to thy name, O thou most High. When mine enemies are turned back, they shall fall and perish at thy presence.

The enemy turned back, stumbled, and perished when David praised God's name. Furthermore, Paul and Silas received a miracle when praising God with a song.

And at midnight Paul and Silas prayed, and sang praises unto God: and the prisoners heard them.   (Acts 16:25)

Consider some other Scriptures of praise:

Some trust in chariots, and some in horses: but we will remember the name of the LORD our God.   (Psalm 20:7)

[God] inhabitest the praises of [His people].
(Psalm 22:3)

I will call on the LORD, who is worthy to be praised: so shall I be saved from mine enemies.   (2 Samuel 22:4)

Praise Is a Command

Anytime the word *praise* is used in the Bible, it is used in one of two ways. First, Scripture teaches us that praise is not an option, it's a command:

Let every thing that hath breath praise the LORD. Praise ye the LORD. (Psalm 150:6)

Well, maybe you used to praise the Lord and now you feel like, well, you can let someone else do that—someone who is a new Christian in the Lord, or a baby Christian. Let me remind you that praise is not a suggestion; it's a direct command. Perhaps some of you reading this are schoolteachers. If you were to command one of your students to move to another seat, would you mean it as a suggestion? No, it's not as if you're giving the child an alternative. It is a direct command. Likewise, when parents tell their children, "Clean your room," are they making a suggestion? This is the way I grew up. If my mother said, "Clean your room," I could think about it only after it had been done.

> Praise is not a suggestion; it is a command. Let everything that hath breath, praise the Lord!

"Well, Pastor Dan, I am not as emotional as you are." Praise has nothing to do with how animated you are. I concede the fact that few people are as highly emotional as I am. I will give it to you that few are as animated as I am. But here's the thing—you don't have to praise as I do, and I don't have to do it as you do. In my racially diverse congregation, I like to say it like this: "Do the black thing, do the white thing, do the Puerto Rican thing, but baby, do something!" So however you do it, do it! Praise ye the Lord!

This won't be for everybody, but take ten seconds and praise God for what He's done. Praise Him for being a Way-maker. Praise Him for being the Bridge over troubled waters. Praise Him for your right mind. Praise Him for health in your body. Praise Him for everything He's done in your life this week. Let everything that hath breath, Praise the Lord! Praise ye the Lord! Praise is not a suggestion; it is a command. Let everything that hath breath, praise the Lord!

You say, "Well, I'm Lutheran." Doesn't matter. Praise Him! "Well, I'm Methodist." Praise Him! "Well, I'm Catholic." Praise Him! It doesn't matter what tradition has told you. What matters is who God says you are.

Isaiah 43:6–7 says,

Bring my sons from far, and my daughters from the ends of the earth; even every one that is called by my name: for I have created him for my glory, I have formed him; yea, I have made him.

You were created to praise God. You were formed to praise God. God said, "I formed you from My glory." You're not here to just work three jobs and then die. People aren't really living if they haven't praised God. Some of you are exhausted because you work so many hours and still can't pay your bills. You're exhausted, and here is the problem with that: everybody has to have a job, because the Bible says, "If a man doesn't work, he doesn't eat." (See 2 Thessalonians 3:10.) So I understand. But you were not created just to work umpteen jobs. You were not created just to pay the IRS. I don't care when your workweek ends. You may say "TGIF" on Friday, but on Sunday, you also ought to say, "TGIS." Why? Because Sunday is when the week gets cracking.

> You weren't born to be broke. You weren't born to be out on the streets acting like a hot mess. You were born to praise the Lord!

Give the IRS what they need; give your boss what he or she needs; but, on Sundays, give God what He needs. Let everything that hath breath, praise the Lord! Why? Because I was created to do this! I was born to praise God! You weren't born to be broke. You weren't born to be out on the streets acting like a hot mess. You were born to praise the Lord!

Many grown folks don't know what their purpose is. They don't know what they were created for because it hasn't yet been revealed to them. But age doesn't have anything to do with revelation. Children can receive revelations. I have watched children worshiping God with tears streaming down their face. Some were only six years old, but revelation supersedes knowledge. Revelation tells them, "You were born to worship your Creator." That's why I tell people to get to church on time, because if they get there in time for praise, they don't miss giving God what is His. Praise is not a suggestion; you were created to praise God.

Praise Is a Response

The second way *praise* is used is an inspired response. That's when something good happens in your life and you want to praise the Lord. The saints sing, "When I think of the goodness of Jesus and all He's done for me, my soul cries out hallelujah."[4] What they are saying is, when I think of the great things God has done for me, I can't even help it—I just cry out, "Hallelujah!"

Perhaps you've sat in church next to somebody who suddenly said, "Hallelujah!" Maybe what happened was that that person began to think about how no one could make a way as God makes a way. Nobody but God could have done what had been done in his life. So praise is a natural response even at the thought of what God has done in our lives, making us want to respond, react some kind of way, to His blessings. Praise means "to exalt." It comes from a Latin word *exalto*, which means "to magnify," "to enlarge." So in response to what God has done for us, we want to praise, exalt, and magnify Him!

I like to think of praise as a kind of tax on the oxygen I breathe. Right now, I am breathing in as much oxygen as I need, and I consider my praise a tax on that. I praise the Lord because He doesn't have to give me breath in my body; He delights in doing so, and I delight in praising and thanking Him!

So praise God no matter what. Praise Him because you were born to do so. Praise Him because of the wonderful things He has done. (See Psalm 107:31.) And, if life has

---

4. Myron Butler & Levi, "Jesus Saves," © 2007 EMI Gospel. All rights reserved.

knocked you to the ground, learn to praise Him from the floor!

> *Let every thing that hath breath praise the LORD. Praise ye the LORD.* (Psalm 150:6)

6

EXPRESS IT

6

EXPRESS IT

Remember, Judah's victory was promised in the word of the prophet, but it was manifested in the praises of the people. Praise is our response to the actions of God, and it is not a suggestion.

> *For great is the LORD, and greatly to be praised: he also is to be feared above all gods.* (1 Chronicles 16:25)

> *Let everything that hath breath praise the LORD. Praise ye the LORD.* (Psalm 150:6)

How do we praise, though? There are a variety of ways shown in the Bible. Through praying, declaring the Scriptures, singing songs, sharing testimonies, making music, dancing, thanksgiving, offerings, clapping, leaping, shouting, bowing, kneeling, bending, and celebrating.

There are seven original Hebrew words for praise in the Bible, and each word has a different definition. They are yadah, halal, tehillah, shabach, barak, zamar, and todah. In this chapter, I will define and explain these words.

Yadah

Yadah means to extend the hands as an expression of our adoration. Have you ever seen a baby or small child hit a surface with their hands? This is because they often use their hands to express inner emotion. In a similar way, we lift our hands with palms facing away from us as a sign of surrender to God, showing that we give it all to Him; we also extend our hands with palms facing toward us, signifying we are ready to receive from Him.

> *Thus will I bless thee while I live: I will lift up my hands in thy name.*   (Psalm 63:4)

Have you ever noticed that a child doesn't have to be taught how to hit? Kids will just innately hit a person, and their parents have to tell them that they can't do that.

Not too long ago, I was with a mother whose child was hitting her. She said, "Oh, isn't that cute?" And I replied, "No, that's not cute, because he'll grow up to be sixteen, and he'll knock you down flat." The time to correct a child is not when he is sixteen; the time to correct a child is when he or she is little. When a child slaps somebody, they are expressing an inner emotion of anger; their hands become an extension of what's going on inside of them. They don't even need to be able to talk. They don't know vernacular, they don't know semantics, and they don't know how to communicate; but they know how to slap, because it's the natural expression of anger.

Now let me flip the script on you. Do you know why we come into the house of God and *yadah*, extend our hands up to Him? We do it as an extension of something that is going on inside of us. Imagine that you go to church and begin to think about a miracle that God did for you the past week; then, all of a sudden, your hands get connected to your heart, and you throw them up in the air and *yadah* the Lord. When you do this, you are expressing praise to God; you lift your hands up in surrender to Him.

> When I researched what it meant to surrender to God, I found that it doesn't necessarily mean surrendering *to* God; it means to surrender your enemies to Him.

Remember, there are two ways to *yadah* the Lord. One way is to lift your hands with your palms facing outward. You *yadah* God, you praise Him, you surrender to Him. The other way is to extend your hands with palms facing toward you, signifying that you are ready to receive what God has for you. *Yadah* praise involves both of these, so we should not neglect one or the other. If you need something from God, open your hand like a cup. Tell God what you need. Take five to ten seconds right now to tell God what you need. Perhaps you're ready to receive something from God, such as finances, salvation for your children, or your marriage to be put in order. Now say, "God, I'm ready to receive."

The other type of *yadah* is when you throw your hands up with palms facing outward as a sign of surrender. When I researched what it meant to surrender to God, I found that it doesn't necessarily mean surrendering *to* God; it means to surrender your enemies to Him. I surrender those who seek judgment against me. I surrender those who have tried harm to me. I surrender everything I do not understand in my life to Him. I surrender all of it to God. Do you need to surrender some things to God? Go ahead, throw up your hands and surrender some people to God right now.

Halal

The second Hebrew word for praise is *halal*, which is the root word for "hallelujah" and means to boast and celebrate the attributes of God with abandon. It is an abandonment of self and other's opinions to celebrate God.

> *Praise ye the* LORD. *I will praise the* LORD *with my whole heart, in the assembly of the upright, and in the congregation.* (Psalm 111:1)

If you are going to *halal* God, you cannot do it quietly and soberly; it means that you are ready for a party! I recently found out that Hollywood movie stars hire people who know how to celebrate to come to their parties. They hire girls who know how to celebrate. I'm not talking about anyone off-color here, but they are still wild and crazy. They hire guys who don't just stand by the wall but who liven up the party. Although the effect is artificial, guests at the party perceive that excitement is happening all around them. Likewise, when you enter into God's gates with thanksgiving and into His courts with praise, you are called to *halal*, or to get the party started, for Jesus, but unlike Hollywood, your excitement should be authentic.

> You can't go beyond the veil into the Holy of Holies, enter into the secret place where the mercy seat on which God's presence resides, until you first praise Him for His mighty acts, for His excellent greatness.

Now consider this: the word *hallelujah* is made up of the words *halal*, which means to praise, and *jah*, which is a shortened form of God's original name, Yahweh. So when you say, "Hallelujah," "Halal-jah," you're saying, "Praise be to God." So if you really want to be Judeo-Christian, if you really want to get down to your Old Testament roots, you have to say it like this: "Hallelu-*jah*." You've got to emphasize *jah*. In other words, "Praise be to God!" You can't just say hallelujah;

you have to say hallelu-JAH! So say it out loud, as if you want to halal the Lord, as if you want to get the party started— hallelu-JAH! You've got to throw it up to God—hallelu-JAH!

Understand that you cannot worship until you have passed through the courts of praise. Praise is not a suggestion; it is a commandment. *"Let every thing that hath breath praise the LORD"* (Psalm 150:6)! You can't go beyond the veil into the Holy of Holies, enter into the secret place where the mercy seat on which God's presence resides, until you first praise Him for His mighty acts, for His excellent greatness. In approaching God, you have to praise Him before you can worship Him. You must praise Him!

So run to Him, saying, "God, I praise You. You carried me through this week. You gave me a new job, healed my body, and touched my children." *Halal* the Lord! Praise the Lord! Do you know how important the word *hallelujah* is? Let me tell you. Do you know what your first word in heaven will be? The Bible says, *"And after these things I heard a great voice of much people in heaven, saying, Alleluia; salvation, and glory, and honour, and power, unto the Lord our God"* (Revelation 19:1). The first word that will come out of your mouth when you are absent on earth and present with God is *hallelujah*! The first word you will say when you see Jesus is *hallelu-JAH*! The first word you will say when you're on streets of gold is *hallelu-JAH*! Glory to God!

Tehillah

Tehillah means to spontaneously sing a spiritual song of praise. *Tehillah* is used 418 times in the Bible, making it the most used word for praise. Psalm 40:3 says,

And he hath put a new song in my mouth, even praise unto our God: many shall see it, and fear, and shall trust in the LORD.

Imagine you are walking through a grocery store and you have all your groceries, so you go up to the front. The line is a little longer, so you start browsing the candies near the checkout. You just have to have some Reese's Peanut Butter Cups, so you throw them in your cart. You know what they call that? Spontaneous impulse buying, because you didn't go in there to buy Reese's, but when you saw them, you acted spontaneously. Do you know what *tehillah* praise is? It's when you go to church not expecting to praise, but, all of a sudden, you do it! You spontaneously sing a song of praise to the Lord.

It's *tehillah* praise—it's spontaneous. Have you ever made up spontaneous praise songs to the Lord? "Well, Pastor Dan," you say, "I can't sing." But that's not true—everybody can sing. Now, you may not be allowed to sing on stage—but you *can* sing. Sometimes, as I'm driving along, I just make up a song: "Glory to You, God; You have been so good to me. Glory to You, God; You been so good to me." A *tehillah* praise is just a spontaneous song, out of your belly, rivers of living water, to the Lord. (See John 7:38.) As Psalm 98:1 says, "*O sing unto the* LORD *a new song; for he hath done marvellous things: his right hand, and his holy arm, hath gotten him the victory.*"

Shabach

The next form of praise, *shabach*, means to address God in a loud voice, to shout! We do not shout because God is deaf but because He is worthy to be heard above the roar of our life!

Because thy lovingkindness is better than life, my lips shall praise thee. (Psalm 63:3)

When we *shabach* God, we're saying, "I'm choosing to shout louder than the voices trying to speak to me and every negative situation going on in my life." And you begin to shout unto God to drown them out; literally, *shabach* means to submerge the other voices.

Not too long ago, a woman came to visit our church and approached me with a question: "Pastor Dan, why is it that you shout so much when you preach in church? What is that all about? Is it because you think God is deaf?" She wasn't being funny, and she wasn't crazy; she was asking a valid question.

All of a sudden, it hit me. Do you know why most people don't understand why we shout like we do? Because we've never explained what *shabach* means. To *shabach* the Lord means to shout with a loud voice. When I researched what it meant, I found that it means to raise your voice louder than the cacophony of sounds around you, louder than the roar of life. Oh, God! The roar of life. How many of you have something negative going on your life right now? Perhaps, on your way to church this week, the devil was talking in your ear, saying, "I don't even know why you're going to church. I don't even know why you pay your tithes. I don't even know why you're going to give God thanks today in what you're going through."

When we *shabach* God, we're saying, "I'm choosing to shout louder than the voices trying to speak to me and every negative situation going on in my life." And you begin to shout unto God to drown them out; literally, *shabach* means to submerge the other voices. I am not talking about loony voices; I'm talking about the negative voices of your upside-down finances, upside-down kids, and so forth. You say, "God, I'm going to *shabach* You." The louder you praise, the more your negativity will diminish. The louder you praise, the less you will have to worry about what the devil has said. *Shabach* the Lord!

Barak

The next word for praise, *barak*, means to bend or bow down to the knees to bless God.

> *O come, let us worship and bow down: let us kneel before the* LORD *our maker.*　　　　　(Psalm 95:6)

Most of the members in my church know that I love the land of Israel. In fact, I recently came back from my sixth tour of the Holy Land, and I am going back to Israel next year. One of my favorite experiences is seeing the Orthodox Jewish rabbis standing at the Wailing Wall or the Western Wall in Jerusalem, crying out for the Messiah to come.

When you *barak* the Lord, you bow down all the way to your knees. Young men go to the Wailing Wall to *barak* the Lord. They are weeping, crying, for their Messiah to come. They are "baraking" the Lord. Now, can you imagine the passion and emotion in which they do that, praying for their deliverer to come? Now, if they can *barak* the Lord that way, without even knowing Jesus, how much more ought we, who have the Redeemer in our lives, *barak* the Lord?

Zamar

The next word for praise is *zamar*, which means to play an instrument unto the Lord.

> *Praise the* LORD *with harp: sing unto him with the psaltery and an instrument of ten strings.*   (Psalm 33:2)

To *zamar* means to praise the Lord with an instrument—high-sounding cymbals and stringed instruments and organs. "Well, Pastor Dan, that's one praise I can't give God, because I don't know how to play an instrument." Incorrect. Did you know that the Jewish people consider our ten fingers to be like strings on a guitar? Our hands are instruments of praise. Psalm 47:1 says, "*Clap your hands, all ye people; shout unto God with the voice of triumph.*"

In America, we have made hand-clapping more about theatrical approval, as in applause, rather than seeing it as a way to praise God. Use your hands as a praise weapon, clapping your hands to give God praise. Let it be an expression of thanks, an overflow of the heart for all that God's done in your life.

However, when you praise God, don't limit it to just clapping your hands. Now there are times when I just clap and don't say anything, because I'm trying to train myself to *zamar*. But I realize that my whole body is an instrument—my heart, my hands, my voice. So I clap my hands and say, "Hallelujah. Praise the Lord. Thank You, Jesus."

Now, free your hands and do this right where you are. Open your mouth and charge the atmosphere! Say, "Hallelujah, praise the Lord. Thank You, Jesus! Glory! Hallelujah!" Praise the Lord! Let everything that hath breath, *zamar*! Praise the Lord!

> Use your hands as a praise weapon, clapping your hands to give God praise. Let it be an expression of thanks, an overflow of the heart for all that God's done in your life.

Todah

Finally, there is *todah* praise, which is similar to *yadah*. It means to give an offering of thanksgiving. In the Old Testament, worshippers would bring an animal to sacrifice to the Lord, praising Him while the animal cooked. In other words, praise cost the worshipper something! When we give an offering, we are not just throwing money into a plate, we are performing todah praise.

> *I am under vows to you, my God; I will present my thank offerings to you.*   (Psalm 56:12 NIV)

Some just yadah, yadah, yadah (talk about it), while others *todah* and "be about it."

A child's life is molded by observation. What he sees you and others do will shape who and what he becomes. What better example will the next generation have than if we don't just talk about the different kinds of praise but also do them? I want to teach the next generation that praise is what I do!

I end this chapter with a scriptural command to praise the Lord in a multitude of ways:

> *Praise ye the* LORD. *Praise God in his sanctuary: praise him in the firmament of his power. Praise him for his mighty acts: praise him according to his excellent greatness. Praise him with the sound of the trumpet: praise him with the psaltery and harp. Praise him with the timbrel and dance: praise him with stringed instruments and organs. Praise him upon the loud cymbals: praise him upon the high sounding cymbals. Let every thing that hath breath praise the* LORD. *Praise ye the* LORD.*
>   (Psalm 150:1–6)

7

PRAISE:
MY WEAPON
AGAINST FEAR

7

PRAISE: MY WEAPON AGAINST FEAR

"Verily, verily, I say unto you, He that believeth on me, the works that I do shall he do also; and greater works than these shall he do; because I go unto my Father."

(John 14:12)

When Jesus said those words, what He was saying, in effect, was "the best is yet to come." You might think that the best things of God were to be found in the days when Jesus walked the earth. But according to Jesus, that is not so. Better things were to come. Why? Because Jesus was going to His Father to make them available to us.

Things with God only get better. That is true for you. As a child of God, your life should be on an upward trajectory. The "*greater works*" that Jesus referred to means that you should be experiencing "greater" in your health, your family, your finances, your career—everywhere. You need to understand that because Jesus went to the Father, "greater" is coming your way. The only catch is this: you have to make sure that your house is in order so that you can receive it. And there is one thing that is poised to keep you from experiencing the greater things of God: fear.

> *For God hath not given us the spirit of fear; but of power, and of love, and of a sound mind.*   (2 Timothy 1:7)

> *There is no fear in love; but perfect love casteth out fear: because* **fear hath torment**. *He that feareth is not made perfect in love.*   (1 John 4:18)

"*Fear hath torment.*" Fear will control your life to such an extent that you can't receive greater.

The Prison of Fear

I recently read a newspaper article about an unusual bank robbery. Walter Unbehaun was a seventy-three-year-old man who hobbled into a Chicago area bank on his cane. He wore no masks or disguises. He just went up to the teller in full view of all the security cameras and said, "This is a hold up. I have nothing to lose." As he said those words, he opened his jacket so the teller could see the silver gun tucked into the waistband of his pants. Walter added, "I only have six months to live and have nothing to lose. I don't want to hurt you."

The teller handed over $4,178 in cash. Walter separated the money into two stacks and stuffed them in his pockets.

> You can
> be bound,
> controlled, and
> manipulated
> for so long
> that the real
> battle you face
> is not outside
> but inside your
> mind. And like
> a criminal who
> has spent a
> lifetime behind
> bars, even when
> you are free,
> you're still
> not free.

It didn't take authorities long to track him down. They had captured his image and license plates and vehicle information on security footage. A few days later, Walter was arrested outside a nearby hotel room. When they asked him why he had done it, Walter told them that he wanted to do something that would guarantee that he would spend the rest of his life in prison, and he knew that robbing a bank with a loaded gun would accomplish that. You see, Walter had spent most of his life in and out of prison. He had recently been released from a ten-year jail term in South Carolina. They had sent him north hoping that he would be able to get his life back together. Yet, instead of enjoying freedom for the last years of his life, all Walter could think about was going back to prison. He said that he wanted to go back because he "felt more comfortable in prison than out."[5]

5. http://www.theguardian.com/world/2013/feb/13/73-year-old-bank-robber (accessed January 22, 2016).

This story may sound crazy to you, but in the world of law enforcement, it is a very common occurrence. Inmates can get so used to the restrictive and regimented life inside prison that when they are suddenly released, the freedoms and choices that you and I take for granted scares them to death. They don't know how to deal with it.

The same things can exist in the prison of your mind. You can be bound, controlled, and manipulated for so long that the real battle you face is not outside but inside your mind. And like a criminal who has spent a lifetime behind bars, even when you are free, you're still not free.

I've seen women who were rescued after years of being the victims of domestic abuse return to their abusive homes because their horrible situations felt safer to them than freedom. When you've been used to "bad" for so long you start to believe that you are not worthy of anything better. You stop seeing yourself as someone who is worthy of being loved. You believe that "bad" is what you deserve. You put up with "bad." You settle for "ok." "Good enough" becomes good enough.

God's "greater" is knocking on your door, but fear has you settling for a life of bondage or defeat.

Good Fear and Bad Fear

There are roughly one hundred thirty-two Scripture passages about overcoming fear. People in the Bible were fearful. Abraham feared a Philistine king would find out that Sarah was his wife. Moses feared leading his people. Peter feared walking on water. Joseph feared prison.

> You can have all the education in the world—and I believe in getting all the education you can get—but until you fear God, you haven't even begun to experience wisdom.

The definition of *fear* is "anxiety, worry, or terror." When you experience worry, you are walking in fear. You may not know how you are going to pay your bills. You may not know what's going to happen with your marriage or your children. But you need to realize that fear, or worry, is from the pit of hell and that praise can help you to deal with fear.

Know this, that you are not alone. We all have to deal with fear throughout our lives. Psychologists say that we are born with two innate fears: loud noises and falling. No matter how old you are, you can be startled by sudden, loud noises and you can experience nightmares of falling in your sleep. But the Bible tells of two other fears. One we are commanded to have. The other is labeled a sin and the Bible says you can go to hell over that fear.

And fear not them which kill the body, but are not able to kill the soul: but rather fear him which is able to destroy both soul and body in hell. (Matthew 10:28)

This is a command to fear the One who is able *"to destroy both soul and body in hell."*

This is the fear of the Lord. It is an honor. It is being in awe of God. This is the reverence that drives us to give our praises to the One who is worthy. Psalm 111:10 says, *"The fear of the LORD is the beginning of wisdom."* This is not referring to knowledge. There is a difference between knowledge and wisdom. There are some people who may have multiple graduate degrees from a university but are dumb as box of rocks. You can have all the education in the world—and I believe in getting all the education you can get—but until you fear God, you haven't even begun to experience wisdom. Serving, loving, and honoring God is the fear of the Lord, and the beginning of wisdom.

> But **the fearful**, and unbelieving, and the abominable, and murderers, and whoremongers, and sorcerers, and idolaters, and all liars, shall have their part in the lake which burneth with fire and brimstone: which is the second death.   (Revelation 21:8)

The lake of fire is hell. How could fear send you to hell? Because it is such an affront to God's trust in your life that He will not share you with fear and distrust. It means that you have lost your faith in God. It means that you have stopped praising Him. It means you have given up. And nothing could be more offensive to God.

Remember all of Job's problems? Many people like to quote Job 13:15 when they praise God: *"Though he slay me, yet will I trust in him."* But that Scripture was not one of praise. Do you know what it was in Job that made him say that?

[Job's] substance also was seven thousand sheep, and three thousand camels, and five hundred yoke of oxen, and five hundred she asses, and a very great household; so that this man was the greatest of all the men of the east.

(Job 1:3)

Job was an extremely wealthy and successful man. By today's standards he lived in a multi-million-dollar mansion on twenty-six acres. But as we know, Job experienced hard times and spiritual attack and lost everything. His health failed and he was covered in boils from head to toe. He took a knife and scraped the skin off of his body. He had three friends who pointed at him and said, in effect, "You must be a hypocrite or else all this would not be happening to you!" (See, for example, Job 8:13; 15:34; 20:5; etc.) His wife said, "Curse God, and die" (Job 2:9).

Yet, in the middle of all his sufferings, in Job 13, he said, "I may have lost everything, but there's one thing I will not lose."

For I know that my redeemer liveth, and that he shall stand at the latter day upon the earth: and though after my skin worms destroy this body, yet in my flesh shall I see God: whom I shall see for myself, and mine eyes shall behold, and not another; though my reins be consumed within me. (Job 19:25–27)

He was saying, in effect, "I know my Redeemer lives, and when this is all over, I shall come forth, because if I lose my faith, houses, cars, and things don't mean anything—they can be replaced—but if I lose my faith, then I am saying that God is a liar, that He is not in control, and that my situation is more powerful than He is." Thus, Job concluded, *"Though he slay me, yet will I trust in him."* And in the end, he received double what he had in the beginning. Why? Because Job decided, "I'll never let go of my faith! I will never stop praising my God!"

Fear of Failure

Everybody I know fears failing at something. An eighty-two-year-old woman in my church recently started her own business. This woman does not have any education beyond high school. But in just a few months, her business quadrupled in size. She recently told me, "Pastor Dan, I done raised my kids, my grandkids, and started on my great-grandkids. Now is my time. When I started out, my grandkids—whom I raised—said, 'Oh, Granny, you're too old to do this.' I told them, 'I raised you.' I listened to everyone's excuses as to why my business would fail, and how I should have done this forty years ago. I'm through listening to people who tell me why I'm going to fail. I started listening to people who are telling me, 'Greater is He that is in you!'"

Do you remember the Parable of the Talents? In Matthew 25, talents are distributed to a group of people. While others took their talents out into the world and multiplied them, the man who received just one talent buried it in the ground. When the master returned he asked, "Where's the talent?" Then man said, "I was scared of you! I thought that if I didn't do something grand with this, something would happen to me. So out of fear I buried the talent. I feared failing and disappointing you!" (See Matthew 25:14–30.)

I may lead a large and diverse church congregation in the Chicago area with a television ministry that reaches beyond that, but I have struggled with feeling like a failure most of my life. Not because I haven't had success but because the spirit of failure has knocked on my door so often. After more than thirty-six years of preaching the gospel and doing ministry, I still never walk in the door of that church thinking, *I've got this!* Most of the time when I stand before a congregation I think, *Oh, God, what if I fail at this? What if I don't say things right?* There are times when I get home after preaching four services and tell my wife, "If nobody comes back next week, it's my fault!" Failure would beat me up so badly. Outside I'd have my happy face on, but inside I felt like a failure.

Then God showed me how to be free from the spirit of failure. One day as I agonized over a service and worried about whether or not anyone would come back, He showed me that all I have to do—all I *can* do—is be faithful with what He has given me. I only need to give Him my best effort with whatever gifts I have. That's it. I can't do any more than that. I need to leave the results up to Him. I've got enough to deal with when it comes down to all the things that are coming at me when I'm preaching at multiple services or leading worship or shepherding the people whom God has given me. That's a lot, but I can handle those things because they are in my control. But I need to stop worrying about how my efforts are received. I need to stop agonizing over the critics and the doubters and the naysayers. All of those things are out of my control. I need to give those things to God and focus only on doing the best job I can with what I have been given.

Once you realize that, deep down in your spirit, you will be free. Then, when the spirit of failure comes on you, you can look back on your life and say, "In that moment, dealing that everything that was coming at me, did I stand for Jesus and do the best I could?" Hindsight may be 20/20 but it doesn't fix anything. Ask yourself, "In that moment did I give it my best effort?"

Now when I leave the church and the devil tries to tell me, "Failure! You should have preached better, after thirty-six year! Failure!" I rebuke the devil by saying, "Fear hath torment, but you're not tormenting me."

Results of Fear

> Fear leads you to excuse and rationalize away God's will and blessings for your life.

Giving in to fear—not the fear of God but the bad fear that causes you to lose faith and lose hope—will cause you to miss out on all the greater things that God has in store for you. Fear leads you to excuse and rationalize away God's will and blessings for your life.

There's nothing wrong with being afraid. We all face fear. Facing fear doesn't mean you're not a good Christian. Giving in to fear is where you fall into trouble. You're going to face defeat in your life. You're going to experience fear of the unknown. Like the apostle Peter, you are going to look at the waves and begin to sink.

But when he saw the wind boisterous, he was afraid.

(Matthew 14:30)

Peter's great mistake was not fear; it was his inability to take his eyes off the thing he feared—the boisterous wind and waves—and to put them on Jesus. That's why he began to sink.

I believe another reason God hates it when you succumb to fear is because fear is contagious. It spreads to those around you. Pretty soon, you're not just sinking in the waves, but you are pulling others down with you.

*And the officers shall speak further unto the people, and they shall say, What man is there that is fearful and faint-hearted? let him go and return unto his house, **lest his brethren's heart faint as well as his heart.***
(Deuteronomy 20:8)

This is part of a list of instructions for men going into battle. It's saying that when you go to war, if anyone is faint-hearted, send them home. When in the midst of the battle even one person is fearful and fainthearted, he or she will take out the other brave warriors around them. What God is saying here, in modern terms, is "no punks allowed!" That might sound rough, but in case you haven't noticed, we are in the midst of a battle. Kids are going to hell. Marriages are falling apart. Pastors are committing suicide. Churches are disintegrating. It has never been more important for brave men and women of God to stand up and praise God, because when you do, fear goes away and faintheartedness is over. Fear cannot remain in the midst of praise.

"*There is no fear in love; but perfect love casteth out fear*" (1 John 4:18). The more you praise God and fall in love with Jesus, the less you worry about fear. *What if?* doesn't matter. When you praise God, fear fades away. Fear loses its grip

> The more you praise God and fall in love with Jesus, the less you worry about fear. *What if?* doesn't matter. When you praise God, fear fades away.

because perfect love casts it out.

It's easy to get all fearful just by watching the news each night. It is the philosophy of the world around us to overstate everything and predict the worst possible outcome for every situation. How many people experience anxiety and depression these days because they are constantly bombarded by negative reports of doom and gloom. Do you remember the Y2K scare? The media had everyone believing that the banks and credit cards and computers of the world were going to cause mass hysteria. It turned out to be a whole lot of nothing. Of course, I'm not saying that there is nothing to fear in the world. We face dangers every day in the forms of diseases, crime, financial fraud, political incompetence, and global terror. But the people of God are not supposed to fall victims to such fearmongering. We are supposed to have the antidote. And we do: praise!

Philippians 4:6 says,

> Be **careful** for nothing; but in every thing by prayer and supplication with thanksgiving let your requests be made known unto God.

The Greek word translated as *"careful"* means "to be anxious." Children of God are not supposed to be anxious about anything. Instead, we are go to God with *"prayer and supplication with thanksgiving"*—praise! And what is the result?

> *And the peace of God, which passeth all understanding,*
> *shall keep your hearts and minds through Christ Jesus.*
> (Philippians 4:7)

Which leads to the next verse of instruction for defeating fear,

> *Finally, brethren, whatsoever things are true, whatsoever*
> *things are honest, whatsoever things are just, whatsoever*
> *things are pure, whatsoever things are lovely, whatsoever*
> *things are of good report; if there be any virtue, and if*
> *there be any **praise**, think on these things.*   (verse 8)

More than just a portion of a Sunday morning church service, praise is our constant attitude and our secret weapon against the debilitating forces of fear and worry.

Remember, when you fear God, you fear nothing else. But when you don't fear God, you fear *everything* else.

"Be Still and Know"

Be still and know your time will come;
God is mindful of the things that you
have done.
He is not a man—He cannot lie;
Remember, watch until you know your
time has come.

Be not weary in well doing,
You shall reap if you faint not.
It's in due season, the harvest cometh;
Remember, fight until you've gained a
crown of life;

Be still and know your time will come;
God is mindful of the work that He's begun;
And He's not a man—so He cannot lie;
Remember, watch until you know your
time has come.
Remember, watch until you know your
day has come.

8

PRAISE AND THE BLOOD OF JESUS

8

PRAISE AND THE
BLOOD OF JESUS

*"For the life of the flesh is in the blood: and I have given
it to you upon the altar to make an atonement for your
souls: for it is the blood that maketh an atonement for the
soul."*   (Leviticus 17:11)

For us to understand how our praise is related to the blood
of Jesus we have to understand that the word *atonement* means
"to be cleared, freed, and forgiven." To be atoned means that
someone else paid a price that you couldn't pay. It's paid in full.
It's under the blood. What you once owed has been erased.
When it comes to God and our sin separation from Him, you
have no hope of ever paying the debt you owe, no matter how
wealthy you are. You can't discount it or put it on layaway.

Praise God, Jesus stepped in for you and paid the price in full. He atoned for your sin.

> *But if we walk in the light, as he is in the light, we have fellowship one with another, and the blood of Jesus Christ his Son cleanseth us from all sin.* (1 John 1:7)

Power in the Blood

You don't hear many preachers talking about the blood of Jesus these days. But back in my early days, I remember hearing the saints constantly referring to the blood of Jesus. In fact, we used to sing about it in some of our favorite old hymns.

> Would you be free from the burden of sin?
> There's power in the blood, power in the blood;
> Would you o'er evil a victory win?
> There's wonderful power in the blood.
> There is power, power, wonder working power
> In the blood of the lamb.[6]

And there were others.

> O the blood of Jesus,
> O the blood of Jesus,
> O the blood of Jesus,
> It must not suffer loss.[7]

And others still.

---

6. Lewis E. Jones, "Power in the Blood," 1899.
7. Anonymous, "O the Blood of Jesus," *African American Heritage Hymnal*.

What can wash away my sin?
Nothing but the blood of Jesus
What can make me whole again?
Nothing but the blood of Jesus.
O precious is the flow
That makes me white as snow;
No other fount I know;
Nothing but the blood of Jesus.[8]

Here's the thing: the blood of Jesus still works today. I think one of the reasons there is so much legalism and judgment in the church today is because people do not have a relevant understanding of the blood of Jesus and what it does. A clear understanding of the blood makes it easier to understand how folks who have led messed-up lives can still be used by God. You might see a singer in the church and think, *I know what she did two years ago.* You might hear someone preach and think, *I know what that man did ten years ago.* We judge people based on our own knowledge and perception of who they used to be rather than recognizing who they have become under the atoning blood of Jesus.

We all have some junk in our trunk. The Bible says that *"all have sinned, and come short of the glory of God"* (Romans 3:23). But thanks be to God, when the blood of Jesus flows over any man or woman it does this work called *atonement*—it washes sins away as if they never happened. That is the reason we can joyfully sing and preach, even though we haven't always lived perfect lives. The blood of Jesus washed away our sins, once and for all.

---

8. Robert Lowry, "Nothing But the Blood of Jesus," 1876.

Over the years we have sterilized and watered down what is a very bloody gospel but the fact remains that the only reason why we can pray and serve and sing and praise is because of the blood.

Blood Is Life

When the blood of Jesus flows over any man or woman it does this work called *atonement*—it washes sins away as if they never happened. That is the reason we can joyfully sing and preach, even though we haven't always lived perfect lives.

In your natural body, the blood pumping through your circulatory system leaves your heart every twenty-three seconds and filters through your body. You are alive because of the blood. Every organ in your body is fed by it. Every organ is different, but they are all sustained because of the blood. In the church, we are not all supposed to be alike. We are a reflection of what heaven will be—red and yellow, black and white. We all function in different ways, but we all stay alive because of the blood.

Our Bible is referred as a "living Word," because without the blood, it is no different than any other book, such as Shakespeare or the

Koran. What separates the Bible from every other book is that it's alive because of the blood. Muhammad, Buddha, Socrates, Plato, and Shakespeare are not alive anymore. But because of the blood of Jesus, this Word of God is alive.

Unlike in the days of the Tabernacle of the Old Testament, we no longer have to bring a bull or a dove to church with us so that our pastor can slit its throat and dump the blood on the altar. For the Bible says that *"all things are by the law purged with blood; and without shedding of blood is no remission"* (Hebrews 9:22). But all that animal blood in the Old Testament only served to kick sin down the road. It did not remove sin, it only pushed it forward until One could come who was greater than a dove or a bull, One who could pay the price for sin. With His own blood, Jesus paid the price for your sin and for my sin. He became the spotless Lamb of God.

Pleading the Blood

You have to learn how to use the blood of Jesus, which was shed for your sins. Romans 5:9 declares that we are *"justified by his* [Christ's] *blood."* When you are *"justified"* your sins are washed away or forgiven; you've been cleared because of the blood. You are now made righteous because of the blood.

> For he hath made him to be sin for us, who knew no sin; **that we might be made the righteousness of God in him.**   (2 Corinthians 5:21)

Jesus died for the ungodly. You needed the blood of Jesus to take away your sin. It releases you. Sin can no longer have dominion over your life. *"There is therefore now no condemnation to them which are in Christ Jesus, who walk not after the flesh, but after the Spirit"* (Romans 8:1). Why? Because of the blood. But you need to know how to make the blood work for you.

Many states in this country have legalized concealed carry permits for firearms. This is because the second amendment to the Constitution gives citizens the right to bear arms. If you are arrested with a gun and you have a permit to carry it, you can go before the judge and plead the second amendment. You are declaring your rights. If you've ever been in a courtroom, a competent defense lawyer will teach you a couple of things about your rights in a legal proceeding. It can be a scary experience to go before a judge. First the charges against you are read. But thanks to the Fifth Amendment of our Constitution, you as a defendant can never be forced to testify against yourself. When asked a question by a prosecuting attorney, you can "plead the Fifth" and remain silent. You can just say, "I plead the Fifth," and no lawyer or member of law enforcement can force you to say anything that will incriminate you in your suspected crime. You have the

> Justification means that you are made righteous in the sight of God, as if it never happened. In fact it restores all of your rights that were stripped from you.

right to remain silent, because everything you do say can and will be used against you.

For those who have been washed in the blood of Jesus, let me explain what it means to "plead the blood." As a believer, you have a real and natural enemy in this world. Some call him Satan but he has also been called *"the accuser of our brethren"* (Revelation 12:10). As a child of God, you are in his crosshairs. He is out to use God's own rules against you to prosecute you and remind you of every wrong thing you have ever done. This is where praise comes in. We can plead the blood to go before God's throne. When Satan accuses you and the judge asks, "How do you plead?" you can say, "I plead the blood!" When the enemy comes in like a flood, you can stand in worship before God and say, "I plead the blood!"

The charges are real. You are guilty as sin. You deserve judgment and punishment. Romans 5:20 says, *"Where sin abounded, grace did much more abound."* But when the blood has covered you, the prosecutor can say nothing else against you. *"**By his own blood** he entered in once into the holy place, having obtained eternal redemption for us"* (Hebrews 9:12).

The blood of Jesus obtained your atonement, but it did something else, as well. Romans 5:9 says, *"Much more then, being now **justified** by his blood, we shall be saved from wrath through him."* As I said before, to be atoned for is to be cleansed. But that only means that your fine or punishment was paid. Justification is completely different. Justification means that you are made righteous in the sight of God, as if it never happened. In fact it restores all of your rights that were stripped from you. When the blood cleanses and atones, that's all right, but you now need your God-given authority back.

When you pay a speeding ticket, you need to be sure they give you back your driver's license, because you can't drive without it. When you get your license back you get your rights back. Justification gives you the right to sing and praise before almighty God when you mess up. Now you're not only atoned for; you're also justified.

In fact, you might find yourself going to God and saying, "Lord, remember that thing I confessed and asked you to forgive me for?"

But God will only answer, "What thing are you talking about?"

You see, with God and the blood of Jesus, what's forgiven is forgotten, as far as the east is to the west. It's gone. Atonement lets you put the car from reverse into neutral, but justification lets you slip it into drive and move forward!

Applying the Blood

So how do we make this work? How do we plead the blood?

> *And they shall take of the blood, and strike it on the two side posts and on the upper door post of the houses, wherein they shall eat it.*   (Exodus 12:7)

This, of course, is part of the Passover story. Israel had been in bondage for four hundred years. Pharaoh refused to let them go. Moses kept going to him, saying, "Let my people go." Nine plagues came on Egypt—boils and frogs and locusts and darkness and all these terrible plagues. But the tenth and final plague was the death of all the firstborn sons of Egypt.

The angel of death would cover Egypt to take the eldest boys of every family, but God gave Israel a plan to avoid this fate. They were to slay a lamb, collect the blood in a basin, and apply it to the doorposts and above the door. Then, wherever the blood was applied, the angel would not push open the door and go inside. By daybreak, a cry of mourning went up in Egypt because every household that did not apply the blood had lost their eldest boy.

How did they get the blood from the basin to the door? The stakes were life and death. If you were in Israel and you didn't get the blood on your door, the death angel would come in and take your oldest boy. The instructions from God to Israel in this matter were very specific:

> *And ye shall take a bunch of **hyssop**, and dip it in the blood that is in the bason, and strike the lintel and the two side posts with the blood that is in the bason; and none of you shall go out at the door of his house until the morning.* (Exodus 12:22)

Hyssop became their paintbrush for the blood. They would dip it in the basin and then apply to generously to their doorposts. Now you're probably thinking, *That's great, Dan, but I don't currently have any hyssop in the house.*

No problem. Revelation 12:11 says, *"They overcame him by the blood of the Lamb, **and by the word of their testimony.**"* There's the hyssop! Every time you praise God and open your mouth and plead the blood of Jesus over your children, your family, your finances, your health…anything, your mouth becomes the hyssop. Your praises and declarations apply the blood of Jesus all over your life, bringing life and not death.

Every time you praise God and open your mouth and plead the blood of Jesus over your children, your family, your finances, your health... anything, your mouth becomes the hyssop. Your praises and declarations apply the blood of Jesus all over your life, bringing life and not death.

If you have a child acting crazy, you can apply the blood of Jesus over their life with your mouth. If you have bills to pay but no money to pay them with, you can apply the blood of Jesus over your finances with your mouth. In every situation of your life that needs the miraculous touch of God, praise will help you to get the blood out of the basin and onto wherever it needs to go.

How do you plead?

I plead the blood of Jesus.

What you are saying, in effect, is, "Devil, I don't have to answer anymore for the things I have done. Never again! They are covered by the blood."

How do you plead?

I plead the blood of Jesus.

You may have screwed up in life and made some bad decisions. Everybody may know about the jacked-up person you used to be. That doesn't matter anymore. You've been atoned for. You've been justified. You now know about your rights to plead the blood and apply it to the areas of your life that are under attack. Now you have your ministry back. Now you've got the glory back. Now you've got your anointing back. Now you've got your power back.

Praise God!

"In Your Embrace"

And I'll get through the storm.
And I'll get through this night.
Though my heart feels afraid when my eyes
have grown dim and my pathway's obscure,
He knows my way and I'll walk in His path
and I'll trust His plan.
He knows my way.
In Your embrace, I feel the grace that's lifting
me much higher.
Your strength renews my faith and proves the
love of God will conquer eagle's wings,
healing streams.
I stand in strength and power, You raise me
up to succeed, a vessel clothed in honor;

I need to be close to You so I can be one with You.
It's not a matter of time or place, only let me
see Your face.
Through the distance You seem so far, only
let me do my part.
To return, I've got to be close to You.

9

PRAISE IS PROPHETIC

9

PRAISE IS PROPHETIC

Children of God, praise is what we were created for:

> Even every one that is called by my name: for I have created him for my glory, I have formed him; yea, I have made him. (Isaiah 43:7)

> But ye are a chosen generation, a royal priesthood, an holy nation, a peculiar people; that ye should shew forth the praises of him who hath called you out of darkness into his marvellous light. (1 Peter 2:9)

You were created to praise God! You were not created for everything else—everything else is secondary. Your primary purpose is to praise and worship God.

Did you know that praise is prophetic in nature? By definition, "prophetic" means to accurately describe what will happen in the future. So when you praise, you are prophetically describing what will happen in your future. Praise is gratitude for the past and speaks provision for your future! Praise sets up your future, and because it is prophetic in nature, it changes not just some things but everything. And once the flow has started, you had better be ready, because it is perpetual, like water through a pipeline.

So if praise is prophetic, then we need to know about prophecy. Lots of folks want to prophesy, and some people, once they've dropped their "prophetical word," seem to disappear. God's Word doesn't return void, but He does expect us to stay planted. We must stay in position to collect the spoils of our prophecy. So don't give a prophecy unless you are willing to stand by it.

Prophesy Again and Again

Let's look at the life of a prophet who prophesied in so many different ways. Ezekiel prophesied by lamenting and telling riddles and parables; he prophesied by clapping his hands and stomping his feet. Read through Ezekiel and notice how he kept prophesying in hopes that the Israelites would listen to him. He cried, but they didn't listen. He stomped his feet, but they didn't listen. He told parables, but they didn't listen. Ezekiel warned the children of Israel in every way—through warnings of coming judgments, commands, illustrations, riddles, parables, allegories, demonstrations, disputations, laments, and wailing—of the coming destruction, but there were no listeners.

After countless prophecies, Ezekiel was taken to a valley of dry bones, where God asked him, "Can these bones live again?"

The hand of the LORD *was upon me, and carried me out in the spirit of the* LORD*, and set me down in the midst of the valley which was full of bones, and caused me to pass by them round about: and, behold, there were very many in the open valley; and, lo, they were very dry. And he said unto me, Son of man, can these bones live? And I answered, O Lord* GOD*, thou knowest. Again he said unto me, Prophesy upon these bones, and say unto them, O ye dry bones, hear the word of the* LORD*.*

(Ezekiel 37:1–4)

After Ezekiel prophesied, he was instructed to open his mouth and prophesy again, that breath would come into them. Did those bones live again? Yes! He had to speak, or prophesy, first to a dead situation, a hopeless cause, before he saw results; he had to see beyond what he saw in the moment. He was doing an advanced action to a manifest miracle.

You have to keep in mind that one prophesy (praise) doesn't always get the job done. It took one hundred twenty years for God's Word to come to pass in Noah's life, and one hundred years in Ezekiel's life. Praise first, stand second. Praise helps you find ways to stand and stay planted. Someone asked me, "Do you move in the prophetic?" I answered, "No, I stand in it!" Don't move in the prophetic, stand in it!

"Well, Pastor Dan," you say, "I have never heard of anything so ridiculous as prophesying to a valley of dry dead bones, especially after so many times." That's why some of you are broke and living in poverty. That's why some of you don't pay your tithes. You tried that before, and it didn't work. The devil has lied to you. As I said before, I learned a long time ago not to be moved by what I feel but to stand on what I know. I'm

I learned a long time ago not to be moved by what I feel but to stand on what I know. I'm not moved by what I hear—I stand on what I know. I'm not moved by what I think—I stand on what I know.

not moved by what I hear—I stand on what I know. I'm not moved by what I think—I stand on what I know.

Richard Roberts, son of Oral Roberts, who visited my church a while ago, said to tell the people in advance that he was not doing a "feeling" line but a healing line. Many people think that if they don't feel anything, they haven't been healed. I'm not worried about feeling; I'm worried about healing.

The problem with some of us is that we no longer tithe. We used to be tithers but have looked around our church and are satisfied with other people doing it. If this is the case, you're missing your blessing. If 3,999 other people tithe, you are going to be the one broken-down, because you didn't tithe and missed your blessing. "Well, I tried it," you say, "and it didn't work." Ezekiel prophesied again and again!

Prophesy is not something you do only once; it is perpetual by nature. If praise is prophetic, and prophetic is perpetual, then praise, too, is perpetual; it is setting up your future!

When God starts blessing you, you will be almost embarrassed when folks find out, because there will be so much favor. You'll think, *Oh, God, now they are really going to hate me if they find out about all this.*

Years ago, I was broke; I had nothing. My wife, Linda, and I were raising three daughters, I was going to college, and I was also raising up a church with a few members and very few tithers; but then God taught me the principle of sowing. I had nothing, but I started sowing perpetually. I paid my tithes. I never missed paying my tithes. I don't like to call it "paying"— I call it "giving"—so I would give my tithes unto the Lord. I sowed the seed, and today, I am walking in harvest. I am walking in favor from the seed I planted twenty years ago. Haters can talk, people can say what they want, but this is what happens.

I've had everything prophesied to me. Folks would come up to me and say, "I hope this won't offend you, but I want to prophesy." I would say, "Bring it on." Death and life are in the power of the tongue. Now understand that I have not seen everything I've been told come to pass—*yet.* I don't know what will happen with some of those prophecies, because I wasn't the prophet claiming it. But I had to learn how to prophesy to myself. Often, prophets are called not to prophesy to the world but to prophesy to themselves.

"Well," Pastor Dan, "I am not a prophet." Yes, you are! Everybody is a prophet. Now let me clarify: I don't want to be disparaging here in any way, shape, or form; I believe in the fivefold ministry; I believe there are apostles and prophets. The Bible says that the church is built upon the foundation of the apostles and prophets. (See Ephesians 2:20.) I believe that. But you must also know that there are false prophets out there. They do not have a covering or a church home, and they don't pay tithes anywhere; they just charge into churches, giving everybody a word. Now, I'm not an evangelist. I've never been an evangelist. I've been a pastor for thirty-five years, and I guard my sheep by telling them the truth. And I know that there are wolves in sheep clothing. (See Matthew 7:15.) The Bible says that in the last days, false prophets will arise. (See, for example, Matthew 24:24.) You will not know a false prophet from a true one unless you've been taught what a true prophet is. A true prophet accurately describes what will happen in the future. Don't listen to others who aren't living biblically.

Prophesy to Yourself

> Praise is prophetic. When you praise God, you're declaring what He has done and you're thanking Him in advance for what He's going to do.

Furthermore, you've got to learn how to prophesy to yourself. How do you do that? You praise! When you praise, you are prophesying your future. That's why, when you catch this, you won't care what anyone around you thinks about you or says about you. Praise is prophetic. When you praise God, you're declaring what He has done and you're thanking Him in advance for what He's going to do. Praise says, "Thank You, God, for things in the future that You've already done."

Look what happened when Joshua and the Israelites praised the Lord:

> *So the people shouted when the priests blew with the trumpets: and it came to pass, when the people heard the sound of the trumpet, and the people shouted with a great shout, that the wall fell down flat, so that the people went up into the city, every man straight before him, and they took the city.* (Joshua 6:20)

When they praised, the walls came down and all hindrances and blockages were removed. I like how Joshua put a bunch of adjectives in there. It was a *"great"* shout! Lift up a great shout! Hallelujah! When they shouted with a great shout, the wall fell down flat, and they took the city. Now did they take the city first or did they praise God first? They praised God first.

Furthermore, look at what happened when Paul and Silas prayed in prison:

> *And at midnight Paul and Silas prayed, and sang praises unto God: and prisoners heard them. And suddenly there was a great earthquake, so that the foundations of the prison were shaken: and immediately all the doors were opened, and every one's bands were loosed.*
> (Acts 16:25–26)

Again, did the prison doors open first or did they praise first? When they praised first, the prison doors were opened. Praise! Praise first, then take the city.

So praise prophesies the future. It is an advance action to manifest a miracle.

Recently somebody said to me, "Pastor Dan, I'm getting old, I'm getting fat, and my hair and teeth are falling out." And something happened to me; I snapped, crackled, and popped. I said the *s* word really loud—"Shut up!" Some of you held your breath just then. That person replied, "What happened to you, Pastor Dan?" Realize that you're prophesying your future with what you're saying. *"Death and life are in the power of the tongue"* (Proverbs 18:21).

A while ago, I took my mother, Mother Willis, to O'Hare International Airport in Chicago to board a flight to go preach in Germany and Ireland. Now, my mother is no spring chicken. She is seventy-six years old. But her ministry didn't start until she was seventy-one years old, when she looked at all her children and grandchildren and said, "I ain't studdin' [focusing on] none of you all. You can act a fool if you want, but Mama is about to get her ministry on." Prior to that, she had been taking care of her children and grandchildren.

So Mother started writing books, and she just finished her second one. She told me on the way to the airport that she was in the middle of writing her third book. Now when the phone rings, people are trying to book Mother for speaking events. They want Mother to come lay hands on others and pray in tongues. And because she is from the sweat school, she hasn't had church unless she has gotten people to the floor.

She gave me a list of to-dos *all* the way to the airport.

I asked her, "Are you scared about the eleven-and-a-half-hour-flight tonight?"

She looked at me and said, "Scared? The devil better scared! I am headed to Ireland to throw some devils up out of there. I'm headed to prophesy to Ireland, and I'm ready to speak over some folks."

I asked her, "Mother, do you have any pain in your body? Do you need an aspirin?"

"What do I need aspirin for? My God, He's a healer. I am going to preach the gospel."

You must understand that you are a prophet. I can't hear you until you prophesy to you! I want you to catch this. Start prophesying, "Father, I thank You for everything You've brought me through, and I want to praise You because I have more money than I know what to do with. I want to praise You because I want to bless somebody." You have not because you ask not. (See James 4:2.) *"It is your Father's good pleasure to give you the kingdom"* (Luke 12:32).

"Well, I don't believe that, Pastor Dan." Then stay broken-down!

I promise you that once the flow starts, you won't be able to get it to stop. At every corner, you will have a miracle waiting for you. I am so blessed and favored right now. I have not taken a raise from my church in thirteen years, and my CFO, Bub, can confirm that. But I am abundantly blessed because, years ago, I started putting praise in the ground, and today, I have streams of revenue coming in.

A couple of years ago, I traded in my yellow Mustang because I had injured my back and couldn't even get down into it, but I sure did like it. I'm hanging on to youth as much as I can.

You know what somebody said to me, though? A man told me that my back was healed and that he was going to buy me another yellow Mustang.

> Praise is your weapon. It's not a suggestion. You were born to praise God, and it's an advance action to manifest a miracle.

I replied, "When can we do this?" You say, "That's just like a pastor." But no, you're missing it. I went through years and years of nothingness and brokenness, and I learned that you can live like you give or you can give until you live. Do you need a financial blessing? Praise is your weapon. It's not a suggestion. You were born to praise God, and it's an advance action to manifest a miracle. Are you praising God?

It doesn't matter who says what about you. You prophesy your destiny. If you are sick, raise your hands and prophesy your destiny: "I'm healed. I will not be sick any longer. I am healed by the blood of Jesus. I prophesy that I have no pain." If you have arthritis, lay your hands over that area and say, "I curse arthritis. I am healed in the name of Jesus. I have no struggles in my body anymore. By His stripes, I am healed." If you need a financial blessing, raise your hands up and say, "I am ready to receive my blessing now, God. My praise is prophetic." Clap your hands unto the Lord and give Him thanks.

The Power of Prophetic Praise

I'll share one more story of the power of prophetic praise. A year ago, I realized I had a growth on my head. I didn't tell anybody; only my wife knew. Every few days, I'd have her check it. It started on my hairline as a little pin-dot and kept growing and growing until it was about two-fingernail-widths wide. She said that it looked like brown cauliflower, and there was hair growing out around it. I kept laying my hand on it, and every few days, I'd say to my wife, "Honey, look at this thing." Later, the doctor said that he was going to order a biopsy to see what was going on.

When Dr. Roberts visited our church, he told us to lay our hands over the affected area and begin to praise God. He also said not to ask God for healing because Isaiah has already said that with His stripes, we are healed.

So, I began to praise God. "God," I said, "I thank You because You took stripes on your back to heal this growth, whatever it is. It's causing no pain, but it's bothering me mentally, so I curse it from the roots out. I praise You that I have no growth there. I've been delivered." I reached up to touch it, but it was still there; then I reached up again, but it was still there, so I went on with the service. A little while longer, I reached up—still there. I said, "Alright, hallelujah, praise God. Well, it's still there."

I went up to my office and praised God; it was still there. Monday, I reached up and praised God; it was still there. I was claiming the promises of God, which *are yea, and in him Amen* (2 Corinthians 1:20). So I said, "God, I am just going to praise You. I am going to continue to praise."

A few nights later, I got home from church and walked into my house. My wife was sitting on the couch. As I walked in, I felt for the growth, but, "My God," I said, "there is nothing on my head!"

My wife jumped up off the couch, pulled my hair back, and said, "You're not going to believe this, but there is not even a sign that there was anything there. Hair has even grown back in its place!"

There was not a shred, a bump, a discoloration, not anything! Why? Because I praised God in advance. You've got to praise Him before the miracle happens. Praise is an advance action to a manifest miracle.

Furthermore, praise commissions angels to work on our behalf. Angels are only one of the means given to us to go gather the harvest!

> *Bless the* LORD, *ye his angels, that excel in strength, that do his commandments, hearkening unto the voice of his word.* (Psalm 103:20)

> *For he shall give his angels charge over thee, to keep thee in all thy ways.* (Psalm 91:11)

Pray Psalm 91, and send your angels! Angels are dispatched when a believer uses God's Word!

Remember, praise is prophetic, and the prophetic helps you to stand against all odds. Praise is not just for prophesying your future; praise is for helping you to stand in the present, knowing that help is on the way.

"Bridging the Gap"

So glad You came into our lives
And showed us there's no black or white,
Love has no color,
It's plain to see.
Now there's a task that's not so hard
But we all must do our part
To live peacefully.

Bridging the gap;
We won't sit still.
Stand in the gap;
If we won't, who will?

Now there's a job for us to do
Yes, that includes me and you
Hand in hand, together, we'll get it done;
Count on me, right from the start;
I'll take the first step,
Yes, I'll do my part;
Let's let love ring from our hearts.

Now the choice is yours;
There's a world
Hear their cry
There are people everywhere,
Let's just show them that we care
And unite.
And unite.

10

WORSHIP IS
REVERENCE

10

WORSHIP IS REVERENCE

"O Lord, I beseech thee, let now thine ear be attentive to the prayer of thy servant, and to the prayer of thy servants, who desire to fear thy name: and prosper."
(Nehemiah 1:11)

"The fear of the Lord is the beginning of wisdom."
(Proverbs 9:10)

Praise is an advance action that manifests a miracle, and it accurately describes what will happen in your future. Praise is horizontal; it can be given to anyone and everyone. Worship, however, is vertical, and you can worship only one god. Worship is not about if or what God has done; it's about who

He is. Praise can be done from afar, which produces faith. Worship, though, can be done only up close and personal, at the foot of a cross, which produces character.

Worship in Spirit and in Truth

In John 4, we are told that worshippers must worship God in spirit and in truth. Let's look at the story of Jesus and the Samaritan woman in more depth. Verses 3–4 read, "[Jesus] *left Judaea, and departed again into Galilee. And he must needs go through Samaria.*" This Scripture seems to indicate that Jesus was not planning on going in that direction; but all of a sudden, He "*must needs go through.*" Some of you reading this are going through some stuff you "*must needs go through.*" Nobody can stop it; nobody can get you out of it. You must needs go through it.

> Worship is not about if or what God has done; it's about who He is.

In Samaria, Jesus came across this woman and asked her for a drink. Understand the setting here—this Samaritan woman was going to draw water from a well, and Jesus had changed His route to pass by the well. So at Jacob's well, Jesus basically said to her, "If you knew who was asking you for a drink of water, you would have asked Him, and He would have given you living water, which you'd drink and never thirst again." (See John 4:10.) Then Jesus flipped the script on her and said, "Woman, go get your husband." (See verse 16.)

Maybe you remember this story from Sunday school. The Samaritan woman said to him, "Well, Lord, here's the thing—I have no husband."

Jesus said, "You have had five husbands, and the man you are with now is not your husband." Notice He didn't even address the iniquity. He hadn't come to condemn her; He'd came to save her. (See John 3:17.) People will condemn you, but Jesus came that you might have life and that you might have it more abundantly. (See John 10:10.)

The woman replied, "*Sir, I perceive that thou art a prophet. Our fathers worshipped in this mountain; and ye say, that in Jerusalem is the place where men ought to worship*" (John 4:19–20).

Then Jesus gave her a schooling on worship. He basically told her to forget her tradition, because there was now a new way to worship—in spirit and in truth.

> *Woman, believe me, the hour cometh, when ye shall neither in this mountain, nor yet at Jerusalem, worship the Father. Ye worship ye know not what: we know what we worship: for salvation is of the Jews. But the hour cometh, and now is, when the true worshippers shall worship the Father in spirit and in truth: for the Father seeketh such to worship him. God is a Spirit: and they that worship him must worship him in spirit and in truth.*
>
> (John 4:21–24)

Now many people confuse worship with meditation, suspecting that it's only inward. Worship is not like that; it must be done in spirit and in truth. "Well, Pastor Dan, I just read the Word. I am more of an intellectual. I read the Bible, and that's how I worship God." I'm not mad at you—I'm glad you study the Word—but Jesus said that true worshippers must worship in spirit and in truth. See, *"the letter killeth, but the spirit giveth life"* (2 Corinthians 3:6). If all you do is eat the Word and digest the Word, so that you are full of truth, but lack spirit, you won't be able to spiritually digest the Word. Your digestive juices cannot break down the Word without the Spirit, who allows you to absorb life-giving truth. "The letter killeth, but the spirit giveth life."

In addition, did you know that worship is the believer's total response (mind, emotions, will, and body) to who God is and what He says and does? According to Scripture, there are three primary elements of worship—reverence, service, and humility. In this chapter, we'll focus on reverence.

The Meaning of Reverence

Worship is about rightly approaching God. Man, in his fallen state, can never approach a holy God. Think of Moses, who couldn't look at the face of God. (See Exodus 33:12–23.) But the Holy Spirit in us makes it possible for us to approach the cross and worship God!

Worship comes from the classical compound Greek word *proskuneó*. Pros means "toward" and *kuneó* means "to kiss." So, worship actually means to kiss toward God. It is something that requires affection. Think of a husband and a wife interacting in a natural way—they love each other, so they show affection. When you love someone, affection is a natural response. When it comes to God, we worship by acknowledging that He is great, and that awesomeness makes us bow down. *"O come, let us worship and bow down: let us kneel before* the LORD *our maker*" (Psalm 95:6). That makes me think of the song "I Can Only Imagine." I'm not sure what I'll do on that day, but I'm sure some affection will be on display!

To have reverence for God means that you fear Him. It doesn't mean that you fear He's trying to kill you. Some of you have sinned this week, and you haven't been to church for weeks. I know why you'll go next Sunday—because you think that God's going to let an eighteen-wheeler run over your car if you don't get there. God's not trying to kill you; He's trying to save you. If God is good all the time, then all the time, God is good.

> The thief comes to kill, steal, and destroy, but God came to draw you into repentance, to save you, and to change your life.

Likewise, sometimes folks have a hard time figuring out if something is from God or from the devil. It's not rocket science here, kids—if it's good, then it's from God; if it's evil, it's from the enemy. The thief comes to kill, steal, and destroy, but God came to draw you into repentance, to save you, and to change your life. It is not His will "*that any perish, but that all should come to repentance*" (2 Peter 3:9). That's what God is trying to do in your life.

So understand that reverence doesn't mean to fear. "Reverence" comes from the Hebrew word *yare*, which means both "to be afraid" and "to revere." It is used two hundred times in the Bible and means to fear God, as in Psalm 15:4: "*He honoureth them that fear the* LORD." As I said, this is not a worldly fear, which causes one to be afraid, scared, or full of dread. I'm talking about fear as in awe and respect, as we would experience seeing the Taj Mahal for the first time.

When Hurricane Sandy devastated the East Coast, I remember thinking about the awesomeness of God being displayed in the sheer force and power of the storm, which turned entire states into disaster areas. Indeed, we have a healthy fear of the storm that blew down boardwalks on the coastline. We will never forget the pictures of twisted steel roller coasters, demolished houses, and cars floating where children used to play on the beach.

I hear people say that they feel the presence of God from the top of their heads to the soles of their feet, and I think that this must be have been what Moses experienced when he took off his shoes on holy ground. Moses was commanded by God to take off his shoes as a sign of respect to His awesome power. (See Exodus 3:5.) And by doing so, he was reverencing God.

My son, Chad, has a little daughter named Claudia, who just turned a year old. Her mama is Polish, and so I call Claudia my little "Kadonka." I don't know what a "kadonka" means, but it sounds Polish to me. Every time I see her, I say, "Come here, my little Kadonka." It just feels good rolling off my tongue. She's a pudgy little thing; she's got a little thickness to her. So the other day, my wife and I were babysitting her, and it hit me that Christmas was approaching. She was just a little tiny baby last year, so this year, it's really going to be her first one.

Now Kadonka doesn't walk; she runs. I mean, she just runs everywhere. So Linda and I had her the other day, and we put her in the back seat of the truck. As we were driving down the road, all of a sudden I heard her start singing, "I love you, you love me, we're a great, big happy family; and won't you say we love you, too." She loves to sing, and since she knows only one song, she sings it about four hundred times a day. Now she doesn't sing the whole song; she sings just the first line or two and then wants me to sing the rest. So I joined in, and we're singing away, when I noticed that, all of a sudden, she had stopped singing and was saying, "Wow!" "Wow!" "Wow!"

What was going on in the back seat? Then it hit me; it was dark outside, and, for the first time in her life, she was seeing Christmas lights. Every house we'd drive pass, she would say, "Wow." "Woowww." My little Kadonka just kept "wowing." She was in awe of seeing and beholding something so spectacular for the very first time in her life.

> Church isn't about where you are going to eat afterward; it's about acknowledging that God is a mighty God.

What happens to us in Christianity is that we get used to everything God does for us. We come to church and think, *Well, that was no big deal, I went to church, paid my tithes. Let's go to brunch.* Church isn't about where you are going to eat afterward; it's about acknowledging that God is a mighty God. He's an awesome God. He's a good God. He's a great God. His mercy is everlasting. Every now and then, you ought to have such a relationship with God, in which He does something for you, and you're stunned speechless. You just say, "Wow! Lord, Your greatness is unsearchable." Be reverent.

Reverence for God's People

Last, God doesn't demand reverence only for Himself; He also demands reverence for His people. We can't say we love God and be irreverent to His children.

> *Let the elders that rule well be counted worthy of double honour, especially they who labour in the word and doctrine.* (1 Timothy 5:17)

> *If a man say, I love God, and hateth his brother, he is a liar: for he that loveth not his brother whom he hath seen, how can he love God whom he hath not seen?*
> (1 John 4:20)

I cannot love God whom I have not seen and not love my brother and sister, whom I have seen. If I love God whom I have not seen, I love my brothers and sisters whom I have seen. So I reverence, worship, God both by showing respect and awe of Him and by showing respect for my brothers and sisters.

"We Serve a Good God"

All I know is we serve a good God
Almighty;
All I know is we serve a good God;
Picked me up and turned me around,
Placed my feet on higher ground;
When I am weak,
Then God is strong,
Till I can sing the victory song;
All is know is we serve a good God
Almighty;
All I know is we serve a good God.

Job was sick for oh so long
They say the flesh even fell from his bones;
But through it all,
He would not complain
Seems I can hear him say
Above his pain,

Questions come and answers don't;
Problems raining on your last ray of hope;
"Lord, where, why, how, when?"

Let me tell you what to say to keep pressin'—
We serve a good God;
We serve a good God;

Picked me up and turned me around,
Placed my feet on higher ground;
When I am weak, God is strong,
Till I can sing the victory song;
All I know is we serve a good God—
A good God Almighty;
All I know is we serve a good God.

11

WORSHIP
IS SERVICE

11

WORSHIP IS SERVICE

The secondary element of worship is service. The word translated word *service* in the Bible comes from the Hebrew word abad, which means to worship through working, laboring, sacrificing, or serving.

> *Put on therefore, as the elect of God, holy and beloved, bowels of mercies, kindness, humbleness of mind, meekness, longsuffering; forbearing one another, and forgiving one another, if any man have a quarrel against any: even as Christ forgave you, so also do ye. And above all these things put on charity, which is the bond of perfectness. And let the peace of God rule in your hearts, to the which also ye are called in one body; and be ye thankful. Let the word of Christ dwell in you richly in all wisdom; teaching and admonishing one another in psalms and hymns and spiritual songs, singing with grace in your hearts to the Lord. And whatsoever ye do in word or*

*deed, do all in the name of the Lord Jesus, giving thanks to
God and the Father by him.*   (Colossians 3:12–17)

*And whosoever will be chief among you, let him be your
servant.*   (Matthew 20:27)

Service is required of us all. The Lord shows us that even
those who want to be leaders among us must still serve.

*I beseech you therefore, brethren, by the mercies of God,
that ye present your bodies a living sacrifice, holy, acceptable unto God, which is your reasonable service.*
                                          (Romans 12:1)

*Rather, let the greatest among you become as the young-
est, and the leader as one who serves.* (Luke 22:26 ESV)

See, there is no way out of it—*everyone* is commanded to
partake in some form of service to God, and that service is
worship.

When Abraham was walking up the mountain to sacrifice
his promised son Isaac, he said, "I and the boy go to worship."
(See Genesis 22:5.) He was actually going to sacrificially serve
the Lord; he was going to give God something so precious to
him. Romans 12:1 says, "*I beseech you therefore, brethren, by the
mercies of God, that ye present your bodies a living sacrifice, holy,
acceptable unto God, which is your reasonable service.*" Here,
"*service*" means "worship."

Work as unto the Lord

Work is a type of service, or worship. Remember, works
don't produce salvation, but they are a form of worship. This

> Your energy is not wasted when you do the work of the Lord. Satan will sap you of your energy and leave you dry. God, on the other hand, will restore and regenerate you.

type of service requires energy. Everyone, big or small, will use his or her energy for something, because every action requires some amount of energy. Think of your energy as the battery level on your cell phone. Each night, you plug it in to recharge, and throughout the day, the battery life slowly goes down as the energy is used, which will happen regardless of how you use the phone. We all have energy, and we should use it for something positive, such as honoring and serving God. Furthermore, we should teach our children to channel their energy into something positive. Then our labor is not in vain:

Therefore, my beloved brethren, be ye stedfast, unmoveable, always abounding in the work of the Lord, forasmuch as ye know that your labour is not in vain in the Lord.   (1 Corinthians 15:58)

Your energy is not wasted when you do the work of the Lord. Satan will sap you of your energy and leave you dry. God, on the other hand, will restore and regenerate you.

> *But they that wait upon the* LORD *shall renew their*
> *strength; they shall mount up with wings as eagles; they*
> *shall run, and not be weary; and they shall walk, and not*
> *faint.* (Isaiah 40:31)

Think of the story of Isaac and Rebekah. Rebekah was serving one day, watering camels and attending to menial tasks, when she was discovered by Abraham's servant and was asked to become Isaac's wife. In one day, she went from being a servant to being served. Serve, and take pleasure in your assignment; you may be discovered one day.

> *No man can serve two masters: for either he will hate the*
> *one, and love the other; or else he will hold to the one, and*
> *despise the other. Ye cannot serve God and mammon.*
> (Matthew 6:24)

You can't be loyal to or serve two masters. God tells us to serve Him, but Satan wants us to do his will at the same time. What's going to happen is that, eventually, the commands, or instructions, of the two masters will conflict with one another. Jesus said,

> *For whosoever shall give you a cup of water to drink in my*
> *name, because ye belong to Christ, verily I say unto you,*
> *he shall not lose his reward.* (Mark 9:41)

"Reward" is promised to those who serve God. Separation from God and a lake of fire are the alternatives that other instructors offer you! Abraham said, "*I and the lad will go yonder and worship*" (Genesis 22:5); this was sacrificial service. Worship is sacrifice, and sacrifice is worship. Worshippers are not givers with bad attitudes. You may serve without worship-ping, but you can never worship without serving.

After a worship experience, David wanted to render some kind of service to God. He asked, *"What shall I render unto the Lord for all his benefits toward me?"* (Psalm 116:12). When his worship was complete, his desire was to serve and give.

Remember Who You Work For

You have to learn that when you serve God, it has nothing to do with the horizontal; it has nothing to do with you and others in the church. You will always get weary in well-doing if you serve solely for other people.

A lot of people get upset when their service goes unappreciated. For example, suppose a woman is faith-ful to the choir. She is at every rehearsal, spends her gas money to get there, and finds babysitters for the kids. But, eventually, she gets upset and says that nobody appreciates her. Understand that, if you have this mental-ity, you may as well leave the choir now; you may as well not teach Sunday school; you may as well not play in the band; you may as well not do anything. Because here's the truth: sometimes there is friendly fire of people who do not feel appreciated. This is because they are not true worshippers. They don't care about others very much. Other times, folks are worshippers, but they've got their own struggles and issues, and they are just trying to get through them. You have to learn that when you serve God, it has nothing to do with the horizontal; it has nothing to do with you and others in the church. You will always get weary in well-doing if you serve solely for other people. Remember that you are serving God. Then, if you're appreciated, hallelujah; but if you aren't, it's no matter. You're not doing it for others; you're doing it for the Lord! (See Colossians 3:23.) Then your labor will not be in vain. (See 1 Corinthians 15:58.)

One day, while speaking to my son, who is a marine, I asked him what the military taught about friendly fire. He told me this: "In training, there wasn't much they told us about friendly fire, except this: People may dress like you, act like you, and even look like you, but one thing will always set apart the good from the bad. *Listen to the voice.* There will be something deceptive in an enemy's voice, which will always raise a red flag and set him apart."

See, friend, even the Lord knows that there are those among us who serve only for themselves, who seek to deceive. He also knows that you can tell friend from foe through listening to one's voice. *"My sheep hear my voice, and I know them, and they follow me"* (John 10:27). Remember, only what you do for Christ will last for eternity. Do everything unto the Lord!

> *And whatsoever ye do in word or deed, do all in the name of the Lord Jesus, giving thanks to God and the Father by him.* (Colossians 3:17)

"After the Rainfall"

Lord, there've been times, with my head bowed low,
And I was in need of a refuge for my soul;

But in every life, a little rain must fall;
But that don't mean He won't hear your call;
Take courage—the sun must shine again.

After the rainfall, there will be a rainbow;
When the howling winds have ceased,
There will come His perfect peace.

You don't even have to wait for the clouds to part
Calm assurance to receive in your heart;
He will send a rainbow—the sun will shine again.

12

WORSHIP
IS HUMILITY

12

WORSHIP IS HUMILITY

"Let us hear the conclusion of the whole matter: Fear God, and keep his commandments: for this is the whole duty of man." (Ecclesiastes 12:13)

To summarize everything we have gone over: Praise is not a suggestion, it is what we were created for, and it is prophetic in nature. Remember that praise and worship are not the same thing. Praise is the entry in and can be done from afar, and it produces faith in us. Worship, on the other hand, can be done only up close and personal, at the foot of a cross, and it produces character in us. We praise God for what He has done and worship God for who He is. Worship involves three primary elements. The first is reverence, which means to fear the Lord. Remember, you can't reverence God and be irreverent to His people. The second is service, which comes from the Hebrew word *abad*.

> *I beseech you therefore, brethren, by the mercies of God, that ye present your bodies a living sacrifice, holy, acceptable unto God, which is your reasonable service.*
>
> (Romans 12:1)

Abraham went up a mountain to worship by sacrificial service, offering up his own son. Worship is serving, and serving is worship. Take instruction from those with a proven track record of service; they've been at the foot of a cross.

And the final element of worship is humility.

What It Means to Be Humble

> *Likewise, ye younger, submit yourselves unto the elder. Yea, all of you be subject one to another, and be clothed with humility: for God resisteth the proud, and giveth grace to the humble. Humble yourselves therefore under the mighty hand of God, that he may exalt you in due time.*   (1 Peter 5:5–6)

One of the Hebrew words for "humility" is *shachah*, meaning "to bow down" or "to lay prostrate." To the Jews, this outward posture reflects an inner attitude of respect and humility. "*O come, let us worship and bow down: let us kneel before the* Lord *our maker*" (Psalm 95:6).

I am going to go out on a limb when I say that I truly believe more marriages could be saved if people would just humble themselves. Churches would be spared drama if

Worship is serving, and serving is worship. Take instruction from those with a proven track record of service; they've been at the foot of a cross.

people would humble themselves. People would keep jobs longer if they humbled themselves. Proverbs 22:4 says, *"By humility and the fear of the LORD are riches, and honour, and life."* Riches, honor, and life—how do you get them? Through humility.

It's amazing how many people don't realize what humility will bring into their life. Jesus was lifted up on the cross, but not before He was laid down on the cross. There is no lifting up without a laying down. I must decrease so the He can increase. (See John 3:30.)

You say, "Okay, Pastor Dan, where has my favor been this year?" I pose to you this question: Is it possible that your humility has suffered? Perhaps you've got everything else in order. You're reverent to God, you've had the "wow" of God, you serve in ministry, but there's no humility. The Bible says, *"Pride goes before destruction, and a haughty spirit before a fall"* (Proverbs 16:18 ESV).

One morning, I was having breakfast with my wife at a local restaurant we have gone to for years, and shortly after being seated, we witnessed a verbal altercation between a waitress and the owner of the restaurant. The waitress had arrived late for work and, apparently, it had not been the first time that week. She had an incredibly bad attitude; rather than humbly backing down, she became incendiary, cussing at everyone. The boss eventually had enough and fired her on the spot. It was right at Christmas time, and I could tell that the boss had not wanted to fire her; however, because she had been too arrogant to accept his wishes for an apology to the customers, he'd really had no choice but to fire her, and at one of the worst times a person could lose her job. She just refused to be humble and take the low road.

> Humility does not mean thinking less of yourself; it means thinking of yourself less.

You must understand that favor comes into your life not because you deserve it. Sometimes you are late, you mess up, you err, you are wrong, you are out of order; but when you say, "Father, Abba Father, have mercy on me!" your Daddy can't help Himself, and He throws favor in your direction. Why? The Bible says that he who humbles himself shall be exalted. (See Matthew 23:12.) Perhaps you say, "Well, I don't want people to think I'm just weak." People don't think you're weak; they think you're intelligent. It is an unintelligent person who constantly fight for his own flesh.

Humility does not mean thinking less of yourself; it means thinking of yourself less. Some of you have such an inferiority complex that you can't even look people in the eye. I am not talking about this beat-you-up, beat-you-down kind of mentality, with which you can't even raise your head. No, humility doesn't mean you think less of yourself as a person. It just means you think of yourself less often. Because it's *not* all about you. Well, perhaps so-and-so said this to you or did that. Humility recognizes that you shouldn't defend yourself. It makes the choice to step back, be quiet, and humble oneself. In thirty-five years of ministry, I have learned that, by the time you put one fire out, there will be another one, and it seems as if all one does is run around putting fires out. You've got to learn how to let it go and just say, "God, I humble myself unto You. At the end of the day, You're the only One who matters." Humility is the activator.

Humility Through Forgiveness

In addition, we worship God when we obey His command to humble ourselves by forgiving others. I've been reading the prayer of Jabez, in which he pleaded to God,

> *Oh that thou wouldest bless me indeed, and enlarge my coast, and that thine hand might be with me, and that thou wouldest keep me from evil, that it may not grieve me! And God granted him that which he requested.*
>
> (1 Chronicles 4:10)

He asked God to enlarge his territory and concurrently not to cause him any pain. Jabez, are you telling me the larger your capacity to forgive, the larger God increases your territory?

The less you forgive, the more you close your life down; but the more you forgive, whether others ask for it or not, the more you open your life up to receive. God is looking for a vessel who forgives as He forgave.

Some folks wonder why favor never comes into their life. They wonder why they never have more, why they never have prosperity. It's because they never increase their capacity to forgive. The less you forgive, the more you close your life down; but the more you forgive, whether others ask for it or not, the more you open your life up to receive. God is looking for a vessel who forgives as He forgave. When He was on the cross, nobody said a mumbling word; nobody asked, "Would you forgive me?" and yet He said, *"Father, forgive them; for they know not what they do"* (Luke 23:34). And today He says that if He can find somebody who forgives like that, He will give him not just riches but wealth. He will give him favor in his life. The larger you increase your anointing to forgive, the larger your territory becomes. Do you need something from God? Forgive somebody today.

That's just not nicey-nice, name it, claim it, clique it, I am a living witness. Sometimes, the hardest thing to bear in life is when somebody hurts you and never says sorry; but if you can, get in your place at the old rugged cross, bow your knees before God, and forgive that person. If you have to cry, cry; if you have to scream, scream—but do what you need to do. When you get up, the enemy will no longer be able to bind you and keep you down. In the rare event that somebody does loop back around and tell you that he is sorry, you will find a true friend who will probably stick closer than a brother. (See Proverbs 18:24.) Likewise, it's not hurt that will kill you, it's the pride of unforgiveness, or refusing to make things right, that will keep you down.

Linda and I have been married thirty-six years because we made up our minds to liberally use the words "I'm sorry." I've had to apologize for things I didn't think I should be sorry for, because I am a peace lover—I love keeping the peace. *"Blessed are the peacemakers"* (Matthew 5:9). At times, something in me wants to rebel and say, "But *you're* not sorry." However, I kind of like my benefits as a married man. I want to stay married, so I say, "I am sorry," until I feel sorry. I confess sorrow until the feelings come.

A lot of folks think they have to feel sorrow before they can say sorry. No, you should say it first and then the feelings will follow. Likewise, this is why faith doesn't come to some of us. We wait on faith to show up and knock the door down, but first we have to confess it with our mouths. The man who waivers shall receive nothing from the Lord. (See James 1:6–7.) But the man who speaks faith, the man who says "I'm sorry," will experience freedom.

Again, humility is a choice. Jesus made this choice and was crucified on a cross before it was even hoisted up. That's because there is no lifting up without first a laying down.

Humble yourselves in the sight of the Lord, and he shall lift you up. (James 4:10)

Humble yourselves therefore under the mighty hand of God, that he may exalt you in due time. (1 Peter 5:6)

Humility is defined in the story of the centurion, a man who understood authority. He had servants of his own, whom he oversaw and ordered; and, when he needed a miracle, he got one, in large part because of his humility. He said to Jesus, *"Wherefore neither thought I myself worthy to come unto thee: but **say** in a **word**, and my servant shall be healed"* (Luke 7:7). Due to this display of humility, he received his miracle. Never lose a miracle by not humbling yourself.

Also, beware of fake humility. The psalmist wrote, *"Hear the right, O Lord, attend unto my cry, give ear unto my prayer, that goeth not out of feigned lips"* (Psalm 17:1). Fake humility is devoid of gratitude. Gratitude is what destroys fake humility, because it takes the focus off oneself. As I said earlier, humility is not thinking less of yourself but thinking of yourself less.

> Fake humility is devoid of gratitude. Gratitude is what destroys fake humility, because it takes the focus off oneself.

He must increase, but I must decrease. (John 3:30)

Ye hypocrites, well did Esaias prophesy of you, saying, This people draweth nigh unto me with their mouth, and honoureth me with their lips; but their heart is far from me.   (Matthew 15:7–8)

The Mirror of Worship

Worship is a mirror that shows who you really are; it's a real-life picture of you next to a holy God. When you get up close to the cross, where Jesus endured the nails, the piercing of His side, and the stripes on His back, when you get up close and personal to that perfection, you realize how imperfect you are. When we are far away from the mirror of worship, we can see many people in the reflection, but when we get close—when we start worshipping—we can only see one person—our self. All of a sudden, we can no longer blame others for our mess. We can't blame others for what we've done wrong. Others may be in our praise party, in our picture, but when we start worshipping God, there is room for only one.

Until my son came along, I was the only man in a house full of women—my wife and three daughters—and we lived in a house with one bathroom. I spent years of my life knocking on the bathroom door, saying, "Let me look in the mirror." Hallelujah, I have my own mirror now. It may not look like it, but I have my own mirror now. It's funny how many people I can see in my mirror when I praise God from far away. Then I can blame my misery on others. Sometimes, we hold to the stigmas that all church folk are hypocrites, all pastors just want money, and all churches are corrupt. We blame everything on others. When we get into worship, however, when we are up close to the mirror, suddenly we can see no one but ourselves. Our imperfections are put up against the cross of Calvary.

> In Jesus' presence, you have to tell the truth about who you really are. That's why most people don't want to worship, because they don't want to tell the truth about who they really are.

In Jesus' presence, you have to tell the truth about who you really are. That's why most people don't want to worship, because they don't want to tell the truth about who they really are. Remember, Jesus said to the Samaritan woman that the hour had come in which she had to worship the Father in *spirit and in truth*. (See John 4:23.) The letter kills, but the Spirit gives life. (See 2 Corinthians 3:6.) The truth produces character in you.

When I look into the mirror, I see that I am a man of unclean lips. (See Isaiah 6:5.) I can't blame it on others; I have to say, "God, it's just me and You. Now it's no longer horizontal, it's vertical. Nobody's in the mirror but me and You. It's me—forgive me, God! It's me—fix me, God!"

Don't argue with negative people who blame you for everything in this world and in their life. They are not worshippers. Worshippers understand that they have to sweep around their own front door. They have no time to talk about or mess with others. They let the Lord fix them. They say, "Fix me, Jesus! Fix me, Jesus! Fix me, Jesus!" There is no need to struggle with people who look down on others. Understand that they can't see a cross on the hill, because they are looking down. My mentor Bishop Brazier once gave me these wise words of advice: "If anyone tells you that a certain person has spoken ill of you, do not make excuses about what has been said of you. Instead, answer humbly, 'They were ignorant of my other faults, else they would have mentioned those too.'"

I want to conclude with a true story. There once was an art exhibit, and all the most prestigious people were there. Hors d'oeuvres were being served along with fine champagne. Everyone was walking by and noticing a picture on the wall of Jesus on the cross. Some of the passersby mocked Him, while others cheered Him, but no one seemed to take the time to stop and admire Him.

Then, one gentleman stopped and looked at the painting. At the very top of the picture were the words "Seek to find the hidden treasure." Unbeknownst to this man, the artist of the painting had been standing off in the distance all night, watching everyone walk by his painting. As the gentleman stood there, seeking to find the hidden treasure, the artist approached him from the back, tapped him on the shoulder, and said, "Lower!"

Bewildered, the gentleman turned around and then looked back at the painting.

"Lower!" the artist said, as he tapped the man on the shoulder. "Lower!" he said, until the man was on his knees. "Lower!" until he was lying on his back looking up at the painting.

Then the gentleman shouted, "I see it! I see the hidden treasure!" For the artist had painted the picture in such a way that unless a viewer were on his back looking up, he couldn't see the eyes of Jesus looking at him.

Dear reader, like this man, may you find all you need, not in the affirmation of others, but in the One who loved you more than His own life! *"Let every thing that hath breath praise the Lord. Praise ye the Lord"* (Psalm 150:6)!

ABOUT
THE AUTHOR

ABOUT THE AUTHOR

Dan Willis did not exactly envision a life in ministry as a young boy growing up in Chicago. Though he loved the contagious rhythms of gospel music, he never imagined that one day he'd be creating them himself. Yet, from these humble beginnings, developed one of today's leading pastors.

As a young boy, Dan's dreams involved entering the medical field as a neurosurgeon until the fateful day when, at age sixteen, he was called to "temporarily" take over as pastor of a local church. Dan is still there, serving as the senior pastor of The Lighthouse Church of All Nations, in Alsip, Illinois. Never wavering, he took that small ministry of sixteen people and nurtured it into the largest multicultural church on the south side of Chicago, consisting of more than five thousand members. The driving force of Dan's ministry has always been uniting the races. If you look out over the congregation during a typical worship celebration, you will see men, women, and children from over seventy-two different nations.

Confronting the walls of racism and prejudice is never easy, but praise has always been his weapon. Dan is a gifted singer, musician, and producer. He founded a community choir called The Pentecostals of Chicago, a groundbreaking move in 1990, bringing together black, white, Hispanic, and Asian singers from more than twenty Chicago-area churches. This group, now known as The All Nations Choir, has six albums to its credit and has performed with artists from Celine Dion to Kirk Franklin, and on missionary trips to the orphanages of Kingston, Jamaica. Pastor Dan also has two solo albums, the latest being *A Man, His Piano, and His Worship*, a collection of hymns and worship songs.

A celebrated television host, he created and hosted the Emmy Award-nominated *Inspiration Sensation* and *I'm Just Sayin'.* He has traveled the country ministering and teaching men and women through the Starting Line Prison Fellowship organization and has also been a national and international speaker on the topics of music, ministry, racial reconciliation, leadership, and community development.

Dan's previous book with Whitaker House was *Freedom to Forget: Releasing the Pain from the Past, Embracing the Hope for the Future.*